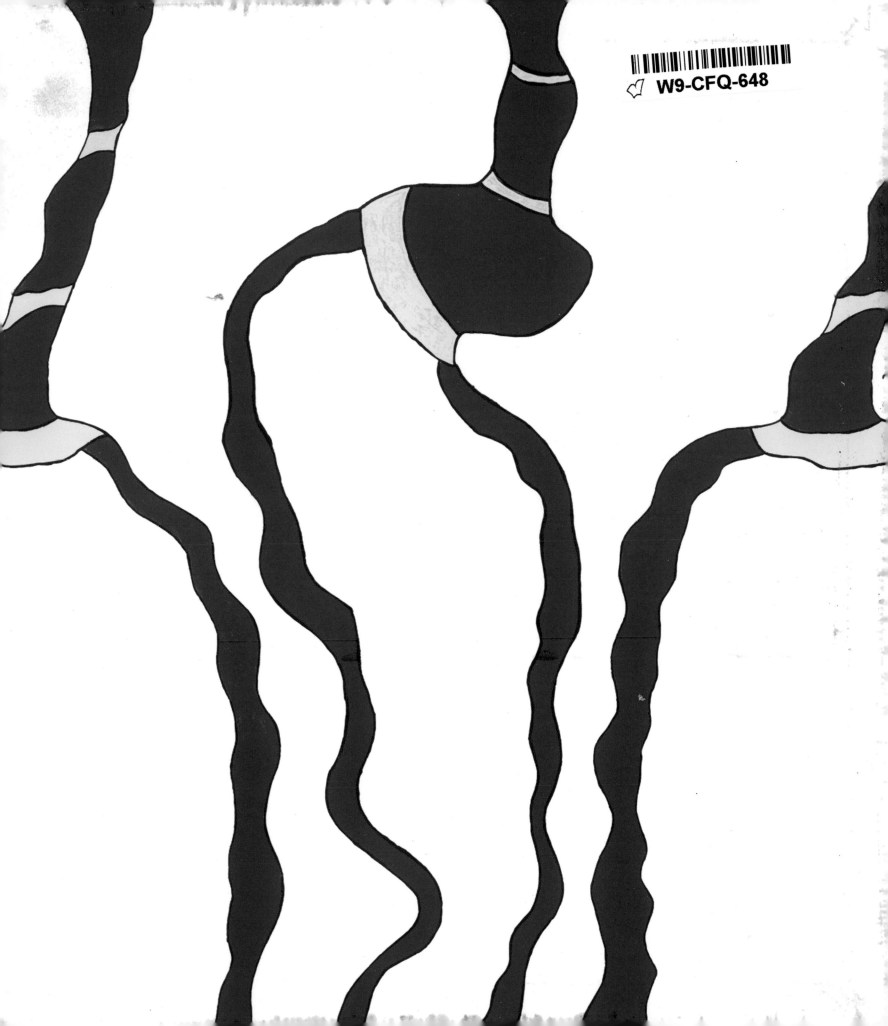

Bangkok
DESIGN

Thai Ideas in Textiles and Furniture

Bangkok DESIGN

Thai Ideas in Textiles and Furniture

Brian Mertens Photos Robert McLeod

Marshall Cavendish Editions

DESIGNER: Lynn Chin Nyuk Ling

Endpaper (front): Untitled, 2005, (detail) by Nim Kruasaeng, acrylic and China ink on canvas,
    180 x 160 cm, photo courtesy of AcaciaFineArt.com.
Endpaper (back): Untitled, 2005, by Nim Kruasaeng, acrylic and China ink on canvas,
    180 x 160 cm, photo courtesy of AcaciaFineArt.com.
Page 2: Red Hallucination, 2004, textile art by Jakkai Siributr.
Photo this page: Traditional Thai tattoo, photo courtesy of Bangkok Fashion City.
Opposite page: Butterfly Screen, 2005, by Pisit Kunanantakul for Isolar.
Page 6: Fake Me, 2002, installation by artist Montri Toemsombat.

Other Marshall Cavendish Offices:
Marshall Cavendish Ltd. 119 Wardour Street, London W1F OUW, UK • Marshall
Cavendish Corporation. 99 White Plains Road, Tarrytown NY 10591-9001, USA
• Marshall Cavendish International (Thailand) Co Ltd. 253 Asoke, 12th Flr,
Sukhumvit 21 Road, Klongtoey Nua, Wattana, Bangkok 10110, Thailand • Marshall
Cavendish (Malaysia) Sdn Bhd, Times Subang, Lot 46, Subang Hi-Tech Industrial
Park, Batu Tiga, 40000 Shah Alam, Selangor Darul Ehsan, Malaysia

Marshall Cavendish is a trademark of Times Publishing Limited.

National Library Board Singapore Cataloguing in Publication Data
Mertens, Brian, 1962-
Bangkok design: Thai ideas in textiles and furniture / by Brian Mertens ;
photographs by Robert McLeod. – Singapore : Marshall Cavendish Editions, 2007.
p. cm.
Includes index.

ISBN-13 : 978-981-232-600-3
ISBN-10 : 981-232-600-6

1. Design – Thailand – Bangkok. 2. Furniture design – Thailand – Bangkok.
3. Textile design – Thailand – Bangkok. 4. Designers – Thailand – Bangkok.
5. Furniture designers – Thailand – Bangkok. 6. Textile designers – Thailand
– Bangkok. I. McLeod, Robert, 1959- II. Title.

NK1478.7.A1
745.409593 -- dc22   SLS2006039300

Printed in China by Everbest Printing Co Ltd

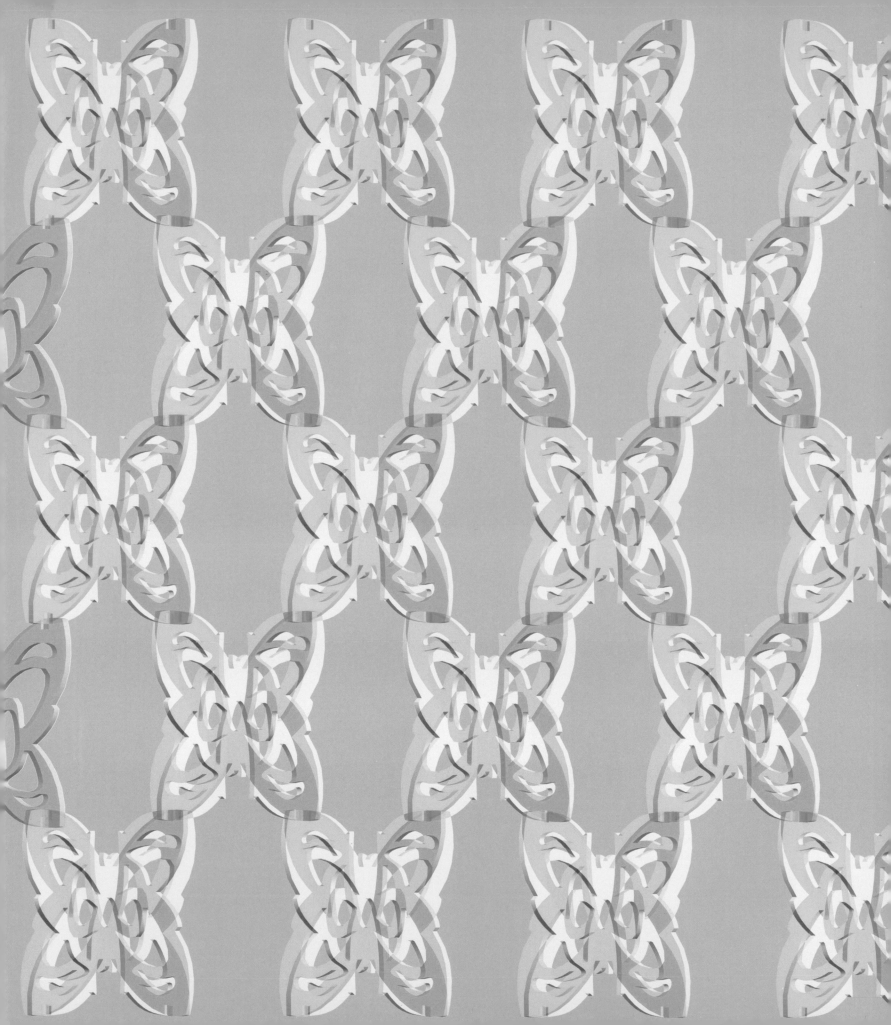

CONTENTS

PREFACE

Photo courtesy of Chanapatana Institute

Where in the world but Bangkok could design be happening in such unexpected ways. Where else except in Thailand would an 80-year-old Buddhist monk establish an academy of fashion and product design taught entirely by professors from Italy. In 2000, Luangpor Viriyang Sirintharo (left), Lord Abbot of Wat Dammamongkol, did just that, founding the internationally accredited Chanapatana Institute, La Scuoloa de Design Italiano, on the grounds of his Bangkok temple. The two-year programme graduates 100 students a year, sending the best on to complete master's degrees in Florence. In recognition of Luangpor Viriyang's project, Italy's president named him a Cavalieri, or Knight, in 2006.

Since the financial meltdown of 1997, Luangpor Viriyang and thousands of other Thais from all walks of life have turned to design to better cope with globalisation. The nation has done this sort of thing before. In the late 19th century, Siam embraced design as a tactic in its strategy for dealing with a hostile outside world. First King Mongkut and then his son King Chulalongkorn built hundreds of palaces, mansions and government buildings in splendid Western styles, to show that Siam and its ruling dynasty stood as peers to the Western powers colonising Asia. This tactic may well have worked—Siam alone in South-east Asia eluded colonial rule.

That architectural legacy, and phenomena like the cavalieri-monk's initiative, are part of Bangkok's uncanny vortex of old and new, East and West, each enhancing the other. On the avenues, the high-rise buildings look like those in big cities around the world. (Modern architecture in Bangkok has yet to come to life the way Thai furnishings and textiles have). But in the side streets and old districts, vital neighbourhood cultures endure. Because the city is populated by so many rural migrants, blessed with a gift for fine handiwork, furnishings companies have been able to produce crafts-based design right in Bangkok.

This social diversity is reflected in Bangkok's evolving design culture. Among the designers profiled in this book are descendents of kings and revolutionaries, sons of rice farmers and shopkeepers, a former punk rocker, even a few foreigners who have put down roots in Thailand. Women are outnumbered by men among designers, but they are well represented among the executives and shareholders of furnishings companies. The premier design firm, The Thai Silk Co., is known by the name of an American man, Jim Thompson, but today it is chaired by a Thai woman. At her firm and other design companies, most of the artisans are women.

The economic shakeup that hit Thailand in 1997, unlike the one in Japan a few years before, seemed to unleash creativity—in business, government, media and many other fields. Some of the best of it happened in design, a field that is unusual in the way it overlaps so many others. Designers tapped their own cultural roots and entrepreneurial drive, sometimes inspired by Royal initiatives in rural development and handicrafts conservation. The government helped with trade shows and product development workshops. Booming inbound travel helped boutiques, restaurants and hotels become showcases for local design.

It seemed everyone in Bangkok was involved in a design-related business. It might well have become yet another Thai crunch—hundreds of new entrants crowding into a niche carved out by a few, strong first-starters. But this time Thai entrepreneurial zeal seemed built on a sense of purpose beyond making money—a sense of meaning and proportion grounded in culture. A certain idealism was at work—a wish to manufacture in a sustainable way, to provide needed jobs, to prove Thailand could make original, high-quality products.

Part of this idealism reflects Buddhist influences, which you can see expressed in aesthetic terms in the design's sense of moderation and balance. But observers tend to overlook the other forces at work in local life, glimmers of the aboriginal spirits that predate Hindu and Buddhist influences. These too animate design, its spirit of improvisation and eclecticism.

Every culture offers its own lessons in how to live. One taught by the Thai way of doing things is how to be sensitive to another person's feelings. Superficially this shows in politeness, charm and the famous smiles. Still better is the high value placed on considerateness. In both their work and personal lives, Thais uncomplacently seek to understand what people really want, and then make an effort to provide it. At its best, this sensitivity to feelings is a spontaneous generosity. Hints of these admirable ways of thinking can, I believe, be seen in furnishings design here—in its will to please.

This book, too, is meant to please, but more than that, to inspire. It is especially intended to serve Thai designers themselves in their efforts to build on this strong first decade of work. It aims also to serve interior design professionals who source products, and to inspire anyone who simply enjoys textiles and furniture. The book is also *about* inspiration, how designers borrow vital elements from their own culture and turn them into ideas for products. Each design here tells its own story. Collectively, the designs tell a big story: that in our increasingly homogenous global age, a global field like design gets interesting when it celebrates local identities, expressed by locals themselves.

As for the book's story, it is a product of my interest in writing about creativity wherever it might be found—in art, culture, government, entrepreneurship, architecture. One of the pleasures of living in New York City in the 1980s and early 1990s was the window it opened to the rest of the world. Movies, art exhibitions, restaurants and performances showed that many of humanity's best creations were being done in Asia. So in 1994 I moved to Tokyo to learn more about Japanese culture. By the 1990s, however, malaise afflicted not only Japan's economy but seemingly the culture itself. A pervasive regimentation, an excess of government, corporate and ideological influence, appeared to be sapping the life out of things at that time. Thailand, where I moved to in 1997, seemed so alive.

Furnishing a Bangkok apartment was not so easy back then, unless you wanted antiques or rustic crafts, generic goods or expensive Italian imports. Ten years later, Thai designers now offer more excellent furnishings than can fit into any single book. The work here represents some of the best, selected on the basis of concept, quality and originality. None of it is cheap, but most of it represents appropriate value. Even very high-end work represents good value for the rare and expertly crafted things they are. Suwan Kongkhunthian's *lipao* designs cost €4,500 overseas, but they are likely the finest woven chairs ever made.

A broader merit is the design's value to society. It is not just the sustainability of so much of this work, its reliance on reclaimed or renewable materials. More than that, it represents the beginning of local efforts to rebalance the often lopsided free flows of globalisation. When end-users buy furnishings from a place like Thailand, where basic monthly wages are just $200 in Bangkok and $100 upcountry, they can help raise living standards. That is because crafts-based design firms tend to provide better pay and working conditions than mass producers.

In fields like product design, Thailand increasingly provides not just its labour and raw materials, but its intellect, enhancing the world's supply of solutions. Thai ideas can enrich us all.

— Brian Mertens

INTRODUCTION

A Sufficient Solution

The contemporary furnishings in this book, all created since the mid-1990s, might seem remote from the elaborate arts and crafts by which the world knows Thailand. This new design has little of the rainbow of decoration that transforms palaces and temples into visions of the celestial. Today's furnishings reflect styles on many wavelengths, but the spectrum is modern and international.

It looks more Thai, however, after taking a new look at the past, as Bangkok creatives themselves are now doing. In the view of architect Duangrit Bunnag, for example, the essence of classical Siamese buildings is not the elaborateness that dazzles the eye, but the thinking inside: "Thai traditional architecture is always produced to achieve a purpose. Sometimes that purpose is very complex, sometimes very simple. But underlying it all is something very sufficient. You know where you have to stop." The structures and decoration of a Buddhist temple, a royal palace or a throne are certainly layered and elaborate, but just enough to achieve their intent of veneration, their symbolism of hierarchy and meaning.

From this vantage, the old Thai way of building things is not over-the-top, not a flight of fantasy, the way it might seem, but quite rational. Likewise the best of the current design, whether minimalist or expressionist, classic or kitschy, does show a sense of reason and appropriateness. It meets Duangrit's definition of being sufficient to achieve its intent. This seems obvious in the case of an understated design like one of ML Pawinee Santisiri's Ayodhya vases (below left), which uses just enough material and craft to achieve the sublime shape of a Sukhothai- or Angkor-period pot, but made from woven water hyacinth rather than stoneware. Similar observations could be made of classics like Suwan Kongkhuntian's Yothaka woven chairs or Sakul Intakul's flower vessels (below right).

But even the quite expressionistic designs embody a sense of purpose. A Saiyart Semagnern piece like The Forest chair takes its particular form because that is what is needed to turn intact, discarded buffalo yokes into a work of art that can function as seating. A Mr. P tape dispenser (below centre) or Mr. P lamp by Propaganda's Chaiyut Plypetch puts just enough form into a piece of plastic to make you smile (and surrender some cash). A design as flamboyant as one of Vipoo Srivilasa's autobiographical ceramics—a teapot built like a sea monster or a figurine of a mermaid dominatrix (opposite)—is over-the-top for a good reason. It makes us wonder, in a way we would otherwise be unlikely to do about a ceramics artist, "Just who *is* this person?"

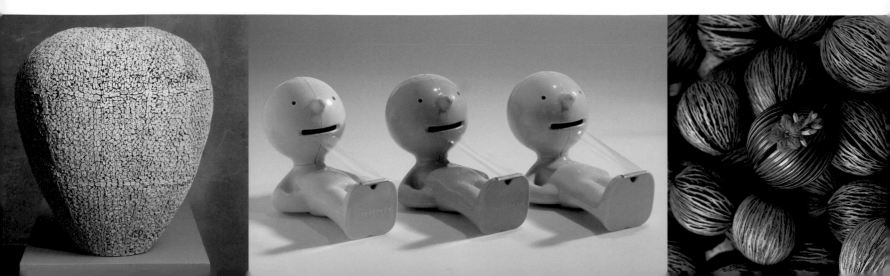

OPPOSITE LEFT: **VESSEL, 2005.** *Water hyacinth, wire frame.* By ML Pawinee Santisiri for Ayodhya.

OPPOSITE CENTRE: **MR P. ONE MAN TRY TAPE DISPENSER, 2002.** *Plastic.* By Chaiyut Plypetch for Propaganda.

OPPOSITE RIGHT: **PONG PONG FLOWER VESSEL, 2002.** *Bronze.* By Sakul Intakul.

LEFT: **MY SEAT, 2000.** *Earthenware.* Vipoo Srivilasa moulds clay into cheeky social critique. His S&M Mermaid figurines parody the repression of gays in Thailand's tradition-bound society. (Photo by Michael Kluvanek, courtesy of Über Gallery, Melbourne)

RIGHT: **KAKANG CHAIR, 2005.** *Rubberwood*. By Suppapong Sonsang for Hygge. Thai furniture designers often favour oblique and acute angles, echoing the trapezoidal geometries of traditional Siamese architecture.

FAR RIGHT: **GULA LIPAO, 2003.** *Woven lipao vine, rattan frame*. By Suwan Kongkhunthian for Yothaka. Some furnishings recall the flowing lines of traditional Thai art and architecture.

OPPOSITE: **TOOTH TOOTHBRUSH HOLDER, PICK-A-TOOTH TOOTHPICK HOLDER, TOOTH LAMP, 1998–1999.** *Plastic*. A Thai sense of fun informs Propaganda's visual puns like molar-shaped containers for dental hygiene items.

Innate Ideas

The notion of sufficiency shows up often in the best design because it is a natural Thai way of doing things, spelled out in the Buddhist ethic of the Middle Way, and written into the unconscious of the culture. Other local traits and attitudes also glimmer through. Optimism and the gift of charm show in designs that are warm, uncomplicated and accessible. They abound in the feeling of *sabai*, easy comfort. Patience and a sense of decorum, *riap roi*, show in neatness and refinement, attention to detail. Siam's cultural eclecticism, proclaimed in temples melding Asian, Middle Eastern and Western influences, echoes in designs that mix city and country, craft and technology, East and West. And all this would be lost without the local sensitivity to aesthetics. "Among peoples in Asia, Thais are a bit like Italians—we are known for being lovers of beauty," observes Schle Woodthanan, creative director of textile powerhouse Pasaya.

Cultural traditions provide a sense of order and structure that can enrich creativity, but what's bewitching about this particular culture is its scope for individuality, independence, improvisation. In furnishings, it shows in an emphasis on individual style. Thai designers do things their way, right down to setting up their own small factories and styling the smallest details of their shops. They take risks. "The word Thai means free. It's in our blood," proclaims Bhanu Inkawat, a pioneering advertising director, restaurateur and founder of

top fashion house Greyhound. "Design here is more vibrant, more creative than in Singapore or Hong Kong because we are more willing to experiment. We're more daring because of this freedom in our way of life. We can do anything!"

While Thai essences and ways of thinking are innate qualities in Thai design, Thai designers also set their work apart by quoting culture explicitly. Thai tradition and everyday life suggest dozens of inspirations for form, function and construction. Eleven of these notions are illustrated in the Local Legacies section at the back of the book (page 172), but they can be seen on every page. Natural materials and traditional crafts, especially the craft of weaving, are the two most important cultural influences. They set Thai design apart because in the rest of the world, mass production and synthetic materials are wearyingly common. Other fresh local influences involve geometry, motif, colour and mood: flowing lines, trapezoids (above left), animal motifs, floor seating and more.

Some designers seek to express local psychology in their designs. Propaganda (page 120), Bangkok's retort to Italian houseware brand Alessi, bases its pop products in *sanook*, the irrepressible Thai sense of fun. Humour comes naturally to Thais like Propaganda co-founder Satit Kalawantavanich, an award-winning director of TV commercials, who finds that *sanook* is as much an asset in design as it is in the Thai advertising films that keep winning the ad industry competition at Cannes.

"WE CAN'T PRETEND TO BE HIGH-TECH LIKE EUROPEANS.
WE HAVE TO GO BACK TO OURSELVES. AS THAIS, WE HAVE GOOD THINGS TO
OFFER THE WORLD TOO, LIKE BEING LAID-BACK. WE'RE NOT OVERLY SERIOUS.
WE'RE HUMBLE, WE LIKE TO SMILE, MAKE NAUGHTY JOKES. WE TEASE EACH
OTHER ALL THE TIME. SO WE PUT THAT SPIRIT INTO OUR PRODUCTS.
IT'S MORE EMOTION THAN FUNCTION," SAYS SATIT KALAWANTAVANICH.

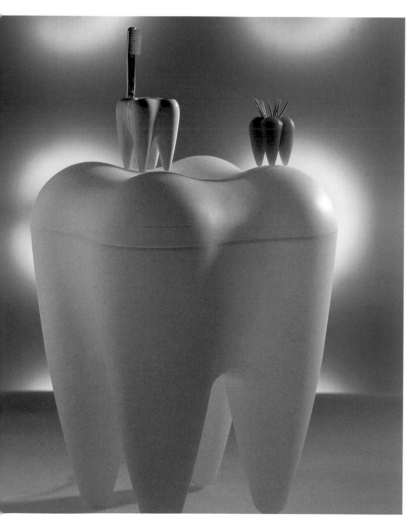

"We know this is not an easy place to make great products," Satit says with a smile both weary and bemused. "There are many constraints here compared with Japan and the West because we are an agricultural society, a low-tech country. The attitude of factories here is not very helpful to design. It's a new thing for them, and they just want high volume. So how do we get beyond these limitations?"

New Symmetries

Thai designers' celebration of *sanook* and other local inspiration fits into a broader Thai movement that began in the early 1990s to forge new identities in culture and enterprise. Pressured by globalisation, the movement is existential (a desire for self-definition) and also practical (a quest for success). It is shaping modern Thai approaches to all sorts of creative endeavors—art, music, fashion, movies, publishing, architecture. "We began trying hard to discover our roots, our own unique offering to the world," says Greyhound's Bhanu. "To me that's very important. We realised that we would not be recognised by the world simply by following the West."

In design, following the West was the way things had been done. When people like Suwan wanted to create modern furnishings with Thai roots in the early 1990s, there were few 'Thai Modern' precedents on which to build. Furnishings

were mostly imported or copied. "We just borrowed Western styles—modernist, Louis XIV. Why? Because we could! It had already been invented for us, so we only needed to copy," says Chatvichai Promadhattavedi, an interior designer, curator and prime mover of the Bangkok Art and Culture Center.

Traditional Thai style, like the classic style that evolved in Bangkok and the central provinces from 1787 to 1932, is hard to modernise because it is so complex in form and meaning. As described in a 1999 study by Chulalongkorn University professor of industrial design Dr Aurapin Pantong, the old style of Rattanakosin—the Thai name for Bangkok—is formal and orderly. It is characterised by symmetry, uniformity and neatness. It features lightness, stillness, ornamentation and the use of multiple, contrasting colours. It implies a hierarchical social order. It adheres to tradition and set pattern, shunning variation.

All this can be stunningly beautiful, as temple architecture shows, but it is difficult to structure correctly when making something new for modern purposes. Designers and craftsmen trying to use Rattanakosin style tend to emphasise ornamentation, neglecting performance. In furniture, for example, the result can be a rosewood chair too massive for a single person to move, with ornate carvings that collect dust. To foreign eyes, and to some Thais too, Rattanakosin style (top left) looks as antique as its Victorian, Continental and Colonial counterparts. And its implicit idealism—its ornamented symmetry and serenity, its painstaking decorum— seems too much for our times.

Steering around these complications, the new design takes an abstract approach to Thainess. It might use bits and pieces of tradition, but not all of it at once. Rarely is it ornate. It sometimes stands the old style on its head. The pots and lamps crafted by artist Thaiwijit Poengkasemsomboon (top right), for example, are asymmetrical and decorated in muddy colours like gray and beige, made out of recycled junk and industrial materials like cement. Each object is a one-of-a-kind sculpture following no set pattern, all but impossible to copy. Thaiwijit's works are as dynamic in form as living things, not still and serene. Yet for all this defiance of the old order, they are quintessentially Thai, evoking the improvised folk construction of villages and Bangkok alike.

Thaiwijit and his fellow designers make their furnishings modern, but modern in a Thai way. Their unique offering to the world comes at a time when some jaded critics and buyers say the West's stylistic options seem all but played out. "When you go to the Milan furniture fair, everybody really looks the same," says Paravi Wongchirachai, knowledge and curatorial director of the Thailand Creative and Design Center. "And nowadays everybody can produce things in China that look like Milan or Scandinavia, but ten times cheaper, and flood the market. So people will pay a premium for things that are unique. That means Thai designers can ditch their insecurity about not looking modern enough, because they can build on the strength of their uniqueness. It lies in all the things we would neglect if we only followed a Western paradigm of design."

Thai ideas are starting to find acceptance among observers

OPPOSITE LEFT: **JIM THOMPSON HOUSE MUSEUM.** Classic Bangkok furnishings like this Chinese-style dining table tend toward the formal and ornate.

OPPOSITE MIDDLE: **FAKE ME, 2002.** Peformance by Montri Toemsombat. An avatar of the new Thai creativity, Montri conducts experiments in performance, installation art and conceptual design that offer questions instead of solutions.

OPPOSITE RIGHT: **POTS, 2004-2005.** *Cement, reclaimed metal.* Painter Thaiwijit Poengkasemsomboon's forays into furnishings design are rooted in both modern art and everyday Thai life.

like *Wallpaper** editor-in-chief Jeremy Langmead. "Whenever I visit Thailand or read the Thai edition of *Wallpaper** I am exhilarated by what I see," he says. "There seems to be an ability to take the tradition and design history that the country has to offer and to give it a contemporary edge with international appeal. Some countries ignore their own roots, which is a shame, or else just imitate what they see elsewhere. Numerous Thai designers seem to be aware of these pitfalls and are coming up with something new, different and yet unique to their culture."

*Wallpaper** established its first Asian-language edition in Bangkok in 2005 thanks in part to the surge in innovation here. Bangkok designers are winning awards like Germany's Red Dot and Japan's G-Mark, and exhibiting in places like Tokyo's Hara Museum and the Pompidou Centre in Paris. The key local trade shows—the twice yearly Bangkok International Gift and Houseware Exhibition (BIG) and annual Thailand International Furniture Fair (TIFF)—have won a reputation as the best in Asia. The strongest designs are coming from a core group of about 100 of the 1,100 firms that show at BIG. Sales of the most successful design brands showed growth of 10 per cent to 30 per cent a year from 1998 to 2005.

This book bows to the individuality of the designs, their strong sense of authorship, by focussing on profiles of 36 featured designers. Many are not designers per se, but fine artists whose work has decorative characteristics. There is even a conceptual artist, Montri Toemsombat, whose installations and experimental textiles comment on sustainability, local cultural identity, and other issues relevant to design. The Local Initiatives section

(page 194) covers other leaders in the evolution of design in Thailand: Jim Thompson; the royal Mae Fah Luang Foundation; the Thailand Creative and Design Center; the pioneers of water hyacinth furnishings; and Bangkok's contemporary artists.

Higher Purpose

The economic motivations to do design seem clear enough—individually, to make a living; collectively, to get into businesses with higher margins and growth potential than the mass production businesses increasingly owned by China. Dr Pansak Vinyartn, the maverick economist who has served as both chief advisor to the prime minister and founder of the Thailand Creative and Design Center, envisions design as a lever to help the Thai economy lift itself from its present value-added model based on assembly production, mostly for Japanese corporations, in which the value added is simply local labour and raw materials. Instead, Thailand will pursue a value creation model that uses local innovation and craftsmanship to produce its own unique products and services.

But beyond economics, do Thais see a higher purpose to fostering design? "Of course there is a higher purpose!" Pansak says. "The essence is not the money. To get money, you don't need design. The essence is to train the mind to be systematic. To explore the mind. To explore the world. To explore the question of freedom."

Or as designer Chatvichai Promadhattavedi puts it, "Creativity means you can write your own brief."

FURNI

FURNITURE | Nithi Sthapitanonda | Ou Baholyodhin | Eggarat Wongcharit | Suwan Kongkhunthian
| Teera Morawong | Udom Udomsrianan | Pisit Kunanantakul | Apirom Kongkanan
| Caryl Olivieri | Swai Silpavithayadilok | Jitrin Jintaprecha | Thawan Duchanee
| Chulaphun Chulanond | Preeda Siripornsub | Saiyart Semangern

NITHI STHAPITANONDA

OPPOSITE: **STATION BENCH II, 2002.** *Reclaimed timber from railway track.* Trapezoidal forms enhance this design, shown at 100 Tonson Gallery.

THE MASTER BUILDER Much of the great furniture of the past 100 years was created either by architects, like Marcel Breuer, or by designer-craftsmen, like George Nakashima. Architects excel in designing well-engineered structures and rational proportions, while the master artisans are admired for the sculptural, poetic qualities of their work.

These two capabilities came together in a sublime 2002 collection of seating, tables and sculpture designed by architect Nithi Sthapitanonda, and crafted by artist Saiyart Semangern. The collaboration shows Saiyart's genius for giving new life to old wood reclaimed from abandoned rice barges, farm tools and railroad ties (page 76). Nithi's designs, meanwhile, contribute harmonious proportions influenced by classic mid-20th century modernism, sometimes with his own playful Thai cultural references.

Years before Nithi had ever heard of Saiyart, he noticed folk imitations of his furniture built by other Thai craftsmen. Nithi, with his architect's eye, felt that this charming craft would be even more appealing if the proportions could be refined. When he finally came upon Saiyart's own seminal designs in an exhibition, Nithi proposed they work together to explore his idea.

"When you see a big piece of teak from an old boat, you get a lot of inspiration. It's different than using steel or plastic. You have to understand the nature of the timber."

Although his furniture has a rustic character, the style Nithi typically employs in his professional practice designing office towers and commercial buildings is pure modernism—sleek and rectilinear, using steel, cement and glass. But his best-known architecture goes beyond International Style to incorporate Thai references. In the early 1990s, Nithi pioneered a successful Thai contemporary style in a series of vacation homes he built in the northern province of Chiang Mai that featured multi-tiered roofs recalling local temples. The construction and floor plan of each house is modern, but the roof structures, extensive use of timber and many decorative features convey a Chiang Mai spirit.

Influential designs like these houses led to Nithi being named National Artist, Thailand's highest cultural award, in 2004. Head of Bangkok's largest architectural firm, A49 Group, Nithi's roots in his profession run deep. His family name, Sthapitanonda, which means architect in Sanskrit, was granted to his clan by King Rama VI in the 1920s to honour a ceremonial pavilion built by Nithi's grandfather. Today Nithi is the architect that any tycoon calls when planning a house.

Nithi says the six months he spent working with Saiyart on furniture allowed him a sense of freedom that is hardly ever possible in his architectural practice, with its constraints of budget, practicality and client requirements. "When you see a big piece of teak from an old boat, you get a lot of inspiration... In my heart I love modernist furniture, but when you play with wood it's different from using steel or plastic. You have to understand the nature of the timber."

OPPOSITE: **STATION MANAGER'S CHAIR, 2002.** *Reclaimed timber from railway track, metal bar.* The muscularity of Nithi's design contrasts with the gracefulness of Pinaree Sanpitak's painting, *pearl offering vessel (2002),* acrylic on canvas, at 100 Tonson Gallery.

BELOW RIGHT: **LOUNGE CHAIR III, 2002.** *Reclaimed makha wood.*

LEFT: **THE FISH-TAIL CHAIR, 2002.** *Reclaimed rosewood.* Several Nithi designs revisit the curvilinear style of mid-century modern furnishings.

"When you want a comfortable chair, you can just go and buy it at the market. Architects love very simple proportions and shapes, geometric forms. It's not nice to sit in, but pleasant to look at. I consider it like sculpture."

FAR LEFT: **BENCH III, 2002.**
Reclaimed teak wood.

CENTRE: **MY GRANDMOTHER'S
DAYBED, 2002.** *Reclaimed teak
wood.* Timber from an old rice barge
is reincarnated as a massive daybed,
260 cm long.

LEFT: **LOUNGE CHAIR II, 2002.**
Reclaimed teak wood.

BELOW: **STATION BENCH I, 2002.**
Reclaimed timber from railway track.
Massive railway timbers take on
appealing proportions in this rugged
design, seen at 100 Tonson Gallery.

OU BAHOLYODHIN
of Ou Baholyodhin Studio

LONDON CALLING The advantage of understatement speaks clearly in the case of Ou Baholyodhin. Pared-down style has helped him become the world's best-known Thai designer. The advantage is not just due to the enduring taste for minimalism; it's also the versatility of this style, which has helped Ou work in a wider range of applications than any other mid-career Thai designer.

Ou has progressed quickly in his profession. In 1997, the year he began designing furniture, he won the *Young Designer of the Year* award at New York's International Contemporary Furniture Fair. Soon he was being asked to design parties, fashion shows and other events for the likes of Kenzo and Madonna. This led to interiors for boutiques in Tokyo and London, and clubs like the K-Bars in Chelsea and Soho. Then came an apartment for film director Tarsem Singh and other acclaimed residential designs as well as a 150-foot yacht.

Working from his London-based consultancy, Ou Baholyodhin Studio, he has made his mark especially in designing interiors for restaurants like Patara, a London hot spot for Thai cuisine. In Barcelona, he designed Lasarte, the base of star chef Passeig de Grazia. Along the way came modern ceramics, lacquer ware, textiles, floral design and two books, *Living with Zen* (2000) and *Being with Flowers* (2001).

Blazing a trail for other Thais, Ou has also done industrial design for large-scale manufacturers, like a premium line of sanitary ware that helped a Bangkok firm launch its own brand, Nahm. That 2002 project was one of the first instances of a big local company hiring a Thai designer to upgrade their wares to compete in an international marketplace increasingly flooded by low-cost goods from China. A year later he created his Time collection of tumblers and stemware for Ocean Glass, the first of several designer lines for that Thai company.

Ou has been creative director for Jim Thompson since 2000, designing their flagship Bangkok restaurant interior, and several furniture collections. His Hemingway series of upholstered seating for Jim Thompson is Ou's favourite among all his designs. With its subtly trapezoidal geometry, these sofas and chairs show textiles to advantage. "Every year I make small adjustments to improve the look, the ease of production or the comfort. I'm very pleased with the final result."

Ou's professional range is the product of his eclectic education. Besides architecture and furniture design, he studied cookery in Florence and political science at the London School of Economics. He's as much London as Bangkok but Asian influences shimmer through in the subtle colours, materials and lines of his designs. "My work is easy on the eye. Nothing loud or brash. There's definitely a feeling of modesty often associated with the Buddhism of Thailand, where I grew up."

"The marriage of East and West has become possibly the most significant theme in interior design."

OPPOSITE: **NESTING TABLES, 1996.** *Oak.*

BELOW: **HK SERIES OCCASIONAL TABLE, 2001.** *White oak, Carrera marble.*

RIGHT: **HK SERIES OCCASIONAL TABLE, 2001.** *Black walnut, stainless steel.*

BOTTOM RIGHT: **HK97 CHAIR, 1997.** *Powder-coated steel, paint.* Asian motifs and concepts show up in most of Ou's designs. His minimalist take on a classic Ming chair was produced in a limited edition commemorating the change of sovereignty in Hong Kong. This one was decorated by artist Erez Yardeni in 2004.

EGGARAT WONGCHARIT
of Crafactor

ART AND INDUSTRY Eggarat Wongcharit's products twinkle with a sense of pleasure and fun because he puts so much thought into them. As one of Thailand's most philosophical designers, he has long been dedicated to process and concept, which reflects the seriousness of his design background. He completed his second master's degree in the renowned product and furniture design programme at Milan's Domus Academy in 1987. After graduation, he spent two years working for leading architect and designer Paolo Nava before becoming a freelance furniture designer in Italy. He returned home in the early 1990s to set up one of Bangkok's first modern furniture studios and to teach industrial design.

"When you design a chair, you have to start with an abstraction, otherwise some existing design will come to mind."

Crafactor is about what Eggarat calls "nifty ideas". Each design tends to have a novel function, concept or look quite different from other products in the marketplace, and is available in a wide range of materials. Because they are so individual, Eggarat views his works as accent pieces rather than sets. He has them made on contract, working closely with specialist workshops and medium-size manufacturers. Eggarat finds this gives him greater flexibility in terms of materials and production technologies than if he were to set up his own factory

Yet production is at the heart of Eggarat's design concept: creating furniture that benefits from an optimal mix of craft and mechanical processes, to better compete in the flood of low-cost mass manufactures from China. It's not enough, Eggarat emphasises, for Thai designers to simply offer nice-looking form.More than

ever before, winning products have to also offer high quality and affordability. Thailand's handmade products are sought-after, but are often too expensive to compete overseas and are sometimes unreliably made.

Eggarat's solution is to design a product whose frame or base can be machine-made to allow consistent quality and lower cost, then cover it with a handmade finishing, like woven materials, to convey Thai beauty, luxury and uniqueness. One example is his Bouncing Betty chair, a braided water hyacinth seat that is mounted on the inflatable inner tube of a car tyre. Cushioning can be adjusted simply by adding or releasing air. The inner tube is the chair's low-cost, mass-produced element, while the seat on top is a piece of handicraft. Eggarat believes so firmly in such a combination of craft and factory production that he proclaims it in his company's name.

PAGE 28: **SYLVIA LOUNGE CHAIR, 2004.**
Stainless steel frame, spandex fabric.
This entertaining piece is named after
Sylvia Kristel, star of *Emmanuelle*, the
steamy 1974 movie set in Bangkok. The
unoccupied chair looks like a drafting
table, but when you sink into it, the planar
surface cradles you like a hammock.

PAGE 29: **SPUTNIK ARMCHAIR, 2002.**
Polyurethane structure, fabric upholstery.
It's named after the Soviet satellite that
launched the Space Age in 1957, but the
Sputnik armchair reminds some Thais of
an antique Siamese coin or Japanese
daruma doll.

OPPOSITE: **GAUDI LOUNGE CHAIR, 2006.**
*Stainless steel tube frame, plastic-coated
wire mesh.* This design is based on
Catalan architect Antoni Gaudí's structural
innovations for the Colonia Guell Chapel,
begun in 1898. (Photo courtesy of the
designer)

LEFT: **ROLLY POLY ROCKING CHAIR,
2002.** *Rattan, fabric, wood structure.*

BELOW: **BOUNCING BETTY CHAIR,
2003.** *Fibreglass structure, braided
water hyacinth, rubber inflatable tyre
inner tube, synthetic leather seat.* The
cushioning of this floor-hugging design
can be adjusted by adding or releasing
air from the base, a car tyre inner tube.

BOTTOM: **ROCK-A-BYE TWO-SEATER
BENCH, 2002.** *Wood, patented mosaic
covering.* Eggarat patented a durable
modern form of mosaic decoration
inspired by the glass mosaic of Siamese
temples and palaces. Here, this material
covers a Crafactor design by sculptor
Paiwate Wangbon.

SUWAN KONGKHUNTHIAN
of Yothaka

TOP RIGHT: **ANTIX BENCH, 2003.** *Woven water hyacinth braid, wood.*

ABOVE: **ZECU CHAIR, 2002.** *Woven water hyacinth braid, wood, rattan inner frame, hand-woven cotton. Gently flowing lines are a Suwan signature that recalls the traditional architecture of his home province of Chiang Mai.*

A SENSE OF *LEELA* Suwan Kongkhunthian's particular mix of life experience has helped him become the most influential of Bangkok's furniture designers, known for his stylistic mastery and for consistently breaking new ground. He grew up amid the temples, teak houses and craftspeople of Chiang Mai, which helped him understand the inner logic of local architecture and design. And as one of the first Thais to practise interior design overseas, he gained an international perspective from a decade working in Singapore.

Suwan focused on furniture ahead of other Thai designers. For his undergraduate thesis project in Silpakorn University's interior design programme, he created a chair. On graduating in 1976 he joined a Bangkok manufacturing firm to become perhaps the first Thai ever to work as a full-time furniture designer.

A turning point in Suwan's life—and in the emergence of Bangkok design—came in 1989 when he returned home to join his classmate and friend ML Pawinee Santisiri (page 84) in founding Yothaka. They were the first designers to launch furniture woven of braided water hyacinth, which they finally succeeded in making popular in Europe in the late 1990s. Thanks largely to Suwan's furniture designs, Pawinee's accessories and their joint entrepreneurship, furnishings woven from this material have become Thailand's signature development in contemporary interior decor (see *Water Hyacinth*, page 210).

Suwan has continued to work with new woven materials. In 1998, he went upmarket—way up—by introducing the first furniture woven from *lipao*. This fine-stemmed reed was previously used only in traditional Thai handicrafts like the delicate baskets that have been fashionable among the

aristocracy since the 19th century. Turning this material into a piece of furniture, like Suwan's award-winning Dalai Lipao chair (page 36), can take a single craftsman up to two months of daily work, hence a €4,500 price tag in European design showrooms. In 2005, Suwan introduced furniture woven from plastic fibre, capitalising on plastic's durability and resurgent popularity. Suwan calls these products a form of 'technocraft', combining hand production with technology. The fibre is factory-made from polyethylene, a type of non-toxic plastic that is fully recyclable.

Suwan's style progresses each year as he launches fresh collections to take advantage of new materials and changing tastes, always in neutral colours and clean but friendly contemporary shapes. True to his experience as an interior designer, the furniture is understated, to harmonise with a variety of architectural settings. Suwan also commissions work by other designers in order to build Yothaka into a furniture house.

Editors and students routinely ask Suwan about his design inspiration, but he believes that a more important question is design identity. "If you don't find your identity, it's very difficult for you to sustain your work as a designer. My work is not specifically Chinese or Thai, but Asian, a mix of regional influences. It shows my own personality, which is 100 per cent Oriental." Ingredients like hand weaving, natural materials and flowing lines provide the Asian flavour. Zen design influence keeps it uncomplicated.

Suwan took years to arrive at his own style. "When I was in school all my professors were overseas graduates, always teaching about Western style, and that's what all my friends were crazy about. I liked it, but it was not in my soul. I still loved Eastern stuff. I only got passing grades. I just didn't realise I was truly an Oriental person."

Designers often talk about lifestyle, but Suwan prefers to focus on *leela*, a Thai word that means grace and control in poise or motion. As Suwan puts it, "Whenever you move, you must have *leela*. Whenever you design, you must have *leela*. If you design a chair for a soldier, you must understand that when he sits in it, his *leela* must show he is powerful. As a leader he cannot slump. When you design for a beautiful queen, the design of the chair must support her *leela*. Form follows *leela*."

"OUR IDEA WAS TO DO SOMETHING THAT REFLECTS OUR ROOTS, THAT SHOWS WE ARE FROM ASIA. IT'S NOT THE DETAILS BUT THE SPIRIT, SOMETHING YOU CAN SENSE. THE MATERIALS AND FORM LOOK ASIAN—A SIMPLE LINE, RELAXING, NOT VERY COMPLICATED. BUT WHEN YOU REALLY LOOK AT THE DETAILS, THERE IS NOTHING RELATED TO ASIA AT ALL. IT'S NEUTRAL, TO BLEND WITH OTHER DESIGNS WELL."

ABOVE: **LORIS LIPAO CHAIR, 2002.** *Woven lipao vine, rattan, timber, hand-woven cotton fabric.* Seen here at Suwan's workshop amid the rice fields outside Bangkok, the Loris chair won Japan's G-Mark Good Design Award and the Hong Kong Design Centre's Design for Asia Award, both in 2004.

OPPOSITE: **MOM DINING CHAIR, 2004.** *Wood, woven plastic.* This chair woven from polyethylene fibre appeared earlier in water hyacinth and *lipao* versions.

PAGE 36: **DALAI LIPAO, 2003.** *Woven lipao vine, rattan, hand-woven cotton fabric.* A Bangok classic that is perhaps Suwan's best design, this roomy, floor-hugging chair won Japan's G-Mark Good Design Award and the Hong Kong Design Centre's Design for Asia Award, both in 2004. (Shown here at Lotus Arts de Vivre.)

PAGE 37: **MOM DINING CHAIR, 2000.** *Woven water hyacinth braid, wood.* Water hyacinth warms up the cement, steel and glass elements of the Oriental Spoon restaurant at the Twin Palms Resort in Phuket.

RETRO PROGRESSIVE Teera Morawong does retro-style furniture not as much for nostalgia's sake as for aesthetic reasons. "Form is the starting point, based on shapes from nature and using ergonomics. It doesn't have to be complex, but it does have to be unique. And yet I don't want a chair that intimidates people. The look should attract them, and then when they sit down, it should be very comfortable. For a table or cabinet, it's about clean lines and function."

Given his concern with form, it's no accident that Teera is drawn to the European-influenced, mid-century modern mode that was popular in the United States in the 1950s and 1960s. Form became the strong point of the era's furniture, as leading designers turned away from the more severe geometry of 1930s Bauhaus style toward biomorphic shapes and a sense of play. The allure of this design reached beyond the United States and Europe. Teera knew it from his childhood in Bangkok during the 1960s and 1970s. Those were the decades when parts of the city became filled with mid-century modern architecture and interiors, a legacy of strong American cultural infuence at the time and because so many Thai architects, interior designers and their affluent clients had studied in the United States. Mid-

TEERA MORAWONG of Allure

"I do retro design because I remember it from my childhood in Bangkok. It has a casual, playful mood that people enjoy in their homes. I love its simplicity, its appeal to the eyes."

CLOCKWISE FROM LEFT:
ANGLE CHAIR, 2002. *Water hyacinth, Thai silk, teak trim.*
CORNER CONSOLE, 2002. *Teak, teak plywood, solid wood frame.*
GRAIN LOVESEAT, 2001. *Water hyacinth, Thai silk, teak trim.*
YMCA LAMPS, 2003. *Metal frame, Thai silk diffuser.*
COMPLEXI TWO SEATER, 2001. *Water hyacinth, Thai silk, teak trim.*
HOLLOW SQUARE COFFEETABLE, 2004. *Teak and plywood.*

DEE STOOL, 2002. *Water hyacinth, wood frame.*

Complete neo-retro ensembles can be put together from Allure elements. Teera adds his own flourishes to mid-century modern style, like the backrest of this blue loveseat, inspired by the form of a grain of rice. The wall sculpture is also a Teera original.

century design had only recently gone out of style in Thailand by the time Teera went to study interior design and business in California in the 1980s. By then Americans, especially on the West Coast, were already reviving the style.

Teera returned to Bangkok to practise interior design in the mid-1990s, and in 2001 founded Allure to produce his own furniture. The retro vogue reached Thailand just in time for Teera to rework it on behalf of fans who liked the look but did not necessarily want to own antiques. Teera's twist on retro is new materials, like woven water hyacinth braid and hand-loomed Thai silk upholstery. Sometimes he Asianises the ergonomics, lowering a seat toward the floor, for example. He uses subtly Oriental lines and cultural references in some designs. The backrest of the Grain loveseat (page 39), for example, is based on the form of a grain of rice; the armrests are set at an angle recalling the decorative finials on the roofs of Thai temples and timber houses.

Teera's designs are popular in the United States, as well as Japan, Hong Kong, Singapore, Malaysia and Thailand. Retro appeals in Southeast Asia because it is lightweight, casual, urban and well suited to the tropical climate. In Thailand, it represents a more middle-class, egalitarian ethos than the other two prevalent Western styles: aristocratic 19th-century European furniture and the Italian modern furniture favoured by the type of Bangkokian who might own a Ferrari. Proof of retro's local appeal can be seen in Bangkok's latest architectural conservation trend. The city's mid-century houses, apartment blocks and hotels are being rescued from the wrecking ball by style-savvy entrepreneurs who turn them into day spas, bistros, dress shops and hotels like Reflections Rooms (page 158).

Teera does up to 20 sketches of a new design before creating a full-size drawing, followed by a model. After years of relying on contractors, he set up his own factory in 2005 in order to work more closely with craftspeople on quality and innovation. He keeps experimenting with new materials, like rawhide and plastic, which he weaves onto stainless steel frames. In the future he wants to move beyond innovating form to develop his own signature materials and techniques. "I want to design at least one piece of furniture that is recognised around the world as a classic during my lifetime. Then I'll truly be happy."

RIGHT: **TANOY CHAISE LOUNGE, 2003.** *Rattan, leather upholstery.* This jazzy design gets its name from the Thai word for a type of ant with a super-oblong body.

OPPOSITE TOP LEFT: **BOOMERANG CHAIR, 2003.** *Woven water hyacinth braid, pine frame, fabric.*

OPPOSITE TOP RIGHT: **HOLLOWAY CHAIR, 2002.** *Vintage fabric, pine frame, teak trim.* Teera put curved ridges on the Holloway chair's backrest to emphasise the figure of the person sitting in it.

FAR RIGHT: **LOOP CONSOLE, 2003.** *Plywood, teak trim.* Slender legs, rounded contours and an open shelf give this cabinet a soft, light look.

UDOM UDOMSRIANAN
of Planet 2001

INSPIRED BY EARTH Udom Udomsrianan is a painter and sculptor by training and a lover of art since childhood. His approach in creating furniture is to embed sculpture in functional objects so that more people can enjoy the pleasures of art. The result is his playful, highly tactile collection based on plant, animal and mineral forms. Strong on intuition, Udom creates furnishings as free-form as sculpture but he dares to put them into regular production, rather than make costly one-offs the way art furniture is usually made.

Udom's animated shapes are a contemporary echo of the design trend toward strong biomorphism that first emerged in Europe and the United States in the 1960s. But Western designers explored curvilinear forms to take advantage of new technologies, like advanced plastics and injection moulding, that could be used to produce almost any shape imaginable. Udom dares to make his furniture organic not only in form, but also in substance, using natural materials like rattan, jute and liana vine.

"Why should furniture just be something to sit on? Why not go inside it? When you were a child, you would take a box and make a room for yourself."

Udom says he takes inspiration from anything that makes people smile or feel happy (modern art, pop culture, cartoon shows like the Jetsons and the Flintstones). But his primary design touchstone is the world of nature. When he first started sketching furniture designs in 2000, for instance, he began with the simple, amorphous shape of a river rock. This became the seat called Form From Mars (page 46). The idea came naturally: "When I can't concentrate or feel depressed, I always think how I'd like to be out in the countryside sitting on a rock by a waterfall. That's the most comfortable moment for me."

Starting from this primitive form, Udom went on to create more complex designs also based on rock shapes. In his third year of work, he put three rocks together to form the Threesome Noodle chair (page 47). A Paris jury awarded this seat a second prize in *Elle Decoration*'s international design competition in 2003. The next year, Udom revisited the rock form, this time deciding to hollow it out so you could go inside. It became a piece of furniture called the Rock Cabin, a kind of cave woven of rattan or liana that provides a private space in which to rest, read or meditate. It's Udom's favourite Planet design: "Why should furniture just be something to sit on? Why not go inside it? When you were a child, you would take a box and make a room for yourself."

It comes as no surprise to learn that Udom worked as an artist before venturing into furniture. He had a typical Bangkok upbringing as one of seven children of a printing shop owner in the city's Chinatown. He spent his school vacations in the countryside, near the old floating market where his grandmother worked as a hawker. Inspired by his father's love of art and music, he excelled at sculpture from a very early age, studied painting at Silpakorn University, and worked as a graphic artist and interior designer before founding Planet. Udom says art school helped him become a better designer. "The professors give you very open-ended questions, and you have to find out for yourself. So this taught me how to think. How do you produce a chair different from what's been done for the past 100 years?"

OPPOSITE: **HALF ORANGE CHAIR, 2003 (DETAIL).** *Rattan, canvas cushion.*

TOP LEFT: **TANK CHAIR, 2005.** *Rattan, polyurethane, cow skin.*

TOP RIGHT: **RING SEAT, 2005.** *Rattan, liana, wood, canvas cushion.*

BOTTOM LEFT: **XYLOPHONE CHAIR, 2005.** *Rattan, liana, polyurethane, stainless steel.*

BOTTOM RIGHT: **BIRDY EASY CHAIR, 2006.** *Rattan, liana, polyurethane.*

Udom says his artisans take naturally to crafting his very free-form shapes.

TOP RIGHT: **FORM FROM MARS SEAT, 2000.** *Rattan, jute.* Based on the primal form of a river rock, this seat became the cornerstone of Udom's subsequent work using curvilinear shapes.

RIGHT: **CRESCENT SEAT, 2003.** *Rattan.* Udom conceived this animated shape from the jade figurine of a *kilin*, a Chinese mythical beast combining features of a dragon and a lion.

BELOW LEFT AND RIGHT: **ROOTED LAMP, ROOTED DAYBED, 2005.** *Rattan.* Udom took his sculptural approach to an organicist extreme in this very large daybed. He applied the form to lighting as well.

OPPOSITE: **THREESOME NOODLE CHAIR, 2002.** *Rattan, jute.* Udom's best-known design, this chair won second prize in *Elle Decoration's* world furniture contest in 2003.

"In the third year, I put three rocks together. I looked at it from every angle, upside down. It reminded me of a mountain I saw in China."

FUTURE ISLAND Heralding the next decade of Bangkok design is a firm whose work might not initially appear to be very local. Modern and softly minimalist, the designs look more Italian than Asian. But a closer examination reveals many Thai ideas. The chairs feature broad seats at low heights influenced by traditional floor seating. There are forms inspired by nature, and lots of trapezoids. Many examples show a sense of *sanook*. Despite some use of advanced materials like carbon-fibre, automotive paints and micro-fibre upholstery fabric, most of the construction is done by hand, not machine. This integration of Thai ideas and very modern design is just one of Isolar's forward-looking faces. Beyond style, the brand belongs to the future because both its talents are, like more and more young Thai designers, formally schooled in industrial design. Founder Pisit Kunanantakul did his degree at the Academy of Art College in San Francisco, as did Apirom Kongkanan, who additionally studied in Italy and Sweden. Isolar is making the most of local manufacturing capabilities, thanks to its parent company, a steelmaking and office furniture conglomerate with some 10,000 employees, owned by Pisit's father. Isolar thus demonstrates how in the future, some of Thailand's

PISIT KUNANANTAKUL &
APIROM KONGKANAN
of Isolar

Industrial Age manufacturers stand to benefit from a Post-Industrial design makeover by the second or third generations of the families that own them. Pisit is also in the vanguard of a likely push by Thai furniture designers into hard-core industrial design: he has created a mobile telephone for one client, and transport equipment for a firm he founded to sell electric cars.

Pisit began sneaking design into his father's company at the age of 14, when he suggested the firm offer its steel office furniture in a broader range of colour choices than the regulation grey or beige. His father obliged with a new product line in red, yellow, blue and other snazzy colours that have sold well to this day. Pisit's design savvy thus confirmed in the marketplace, his father sent him to the United States to get a BFA in product design. On returning

to Bangkok in 2001, he set up Isolar within the family firm to sell designer furniture imported from Italy and to launch competing products designed according to his own tastes.

"Isolar means island. It represents me. I'm kind of isolated, and I like things that other people don't. So this is my island, a personal island, not a common one. But people who want something different can join me there," says Pisit. His work reveals his penchant for technology, futuristic style and fantasy, all of which are very familiar to Thais born since the 1970s who are weaned on anime, video games and sci-fi. A softer touch is palpable in the Isolar designs by Apirom. Her banana-shaped Mooon daybed, for example, done in yellow leather on a wooden frame, shows a sense of playfulness that is a result of her MFA studies in children's product design.

"OUR STYLE IS MINIMALIST, BUT WITH A LITTLE BIT OF JOY—
IN COLOUR, FORM, THE WAY YOU USE IT," SAYS APIROM.

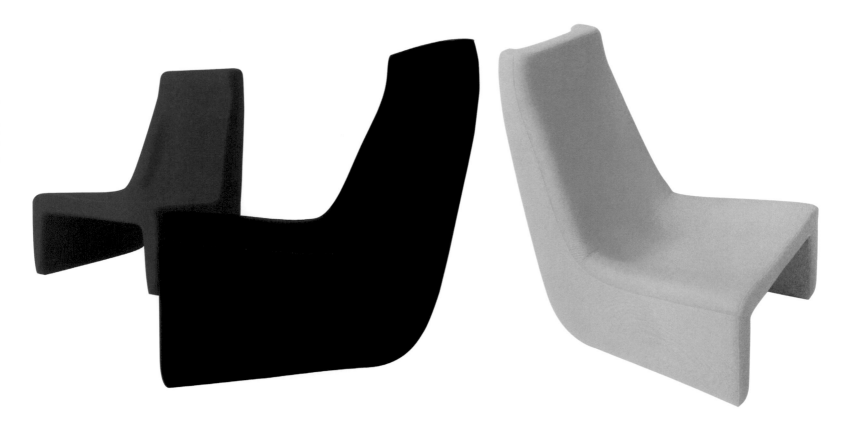

OPPOSITE: **EANE LOUNGE CHAIR, 2005.**
Wooden frame, industrial polyester cover. With its low seat and high back, this chair is one of Pisit's most popular designs.

LEFT: **PLEAT PLEAT CHAIR AND OTTOMAN, 2004.** *Steel base, wooden frame with felt cover.* Apirom's design takes advantage of the soft texture, cushioning and flowing lines of pleated fabric.

BELOW: **BLUNT TABLE, 2004.** *Steel, wood inner core, auto paint.* This table is cutting-edge but with rounded sides and trapezoidal legs, as designed by Pisit.

BELOW: **WIND CHAIR, 2004.** *Ash wood.* Pisit draws his inspiration for this chair from minimalist sculptor Donald Judd.

CARYL OLIVIERI
of Atmosfer and Artitude

AESTHETIC VALUES A rational, European focus on form and concept characterised the design approach of the late Caryl Olivieri, who is known for the contemporary rattan furniture he created with Artitude, collaborating closely with the firm's managing director Voravit Wongkijjalerd. Sticking to concept rather than product helped make Olivieri productive and versatile. His Artitude line, for example, includes five collections, all in his signature minimalist style. Beyond furniture, he designed gardens, interiors and ceramics, and before his untimely death in 2004 he had been planning a lifestyle collection including a fragrance and music compilations for his own brand, Atmosfer.

OPPOSITE: **ARTITUDE SHOWROOM, 2004**

THIS PAGE: **ARTITUDE AND ATMOSFER FURNISHINGS, 2004.**

Olivieri's designs lend a look of stability to a setting, as seen in Artitude's showroom and his own Bangkok apartment.

Rattan furniture has been popular in Thailand for more than 50 years, but it had typically been done in 19th-century European styles in a natural finish or white. Olivieri used local craftsmanship for his Artitude designs, but he shunned the curves of Thai- and colonial-style rattan. Instead he employed a rectilinear geometry—chunky, but cool and architectural. He applied lacquer in muted colours like beige, taupe, grey and cream. A set of Artitude pieces becomes the keystone of an interior in which the furniture lends a sense of order and structure, a quiet complement to room decorations like plants, accessories and art.

Having grown up in Corsica, Olivieri had both French and Italian cultural backgrounds. He studied design and worked as a model in Paris, where he got to know people like Jean Paul Gautier and Christian Lacroix. He later wrote travel guidebooks, living in Brazil, China and Taiwan before coming to Thailand to make jewellery for the Elle brand. Sadly indeed, his promising career was cut short in 2004 when he died from a fall while tending the balcony garden in his high-rise apartment.

Eastern philosophy influenced Olivieri's design approach. He read about Buddhism at the age of 12 and became a lifelong adherent. One of his aesthetic objectives was the Buddhist ideal of tranquility. "Design is only interesting to the extent it can bring more peace and harmony to everyday life through beauty and aesthetics. All my life I've been thinking about that. If you bring people something beautiful, they will, without ever knowing it, become more peaceful in their everyday life."

He also practiced the Buddhist ideal of compassion in his work. He donated exactly 37.9 per cent of his earnings to the Red Cross, breast cancer research, HIV/AIDS programmes and other causes, choosing that figure from his belief that the numbers 3, 7 and 9 are auspicious. At his factory, he paid above-market wages and covered school fees for his employee's children.

"If you bring people something beautiful, they will, without ever knowing it, become more peaceful in their everyday life."

OPPOSITE: **DONA HALF BENCH AND STOOL, 2003.** *Woven rattan, wood, velvet fabric.* Artitude's Voravit collaborated with Olivieri on this characteristic design.

RIGHT: **SILIUM ARMCHAIR, 2003.** *Woven rattan, wood, fabric.* Pure rectilinear designs were Olivieri's forte, like this Artitude piece.

SWAI SILPAVITHAYADILOK
for Hygge

ABOVE: **3 COINS BENCH, 2004.** *Rubber tree wood.* The backrests of this seat can be removed, allowing several different configurations.

OPPOSITE: **EQUINOX CHAIR, 2004.** *Rubber tree wood, fabric.* This design has a complete integrity of its own while evoking predecessors ranging from Adirondacks-style chairs to Richard Riemerschmid's 1900 timber armchair design for Fleischauer's Sons of Nurenberg.

THE REVISIONIST 'Green' products are often stylistically grey, which is one of the challenges for today's designers. One talent who surmounts the task is Swai Silpavithayadilok, who creates rubberwood furniture that is both sustainable and full of wit. With his quiet sense of play, Swai shows how the stroke of a pen can help turn ecologically friendly materials like plantation wood into products that are as stylish as those made from less renewable materials. Instead of using rare materials and complex construction, Swai relies on sophisticated inspiration, an eclectic stylistic referencing, to give his furniture its smart appeal.

High-end timber furniture from South-east Asia is usually made from fine woods, and here unfortunately wild trees are harvested almost exclusively in an unsustainable manner. Swai's designs are instead made from wood grown

in rubber tree farms. Thailand, as the world's largest producer of rubber, has vast acreage of these trees, which need to be cut down when they are about 30 years old after they stop producing latex and die. Many factories have capitalised on the vast local supply of this inexpensive wood, but previously just to make cheap products. The company that makes Swai's work, for example, has been using rubberwood to build generic furniture for decades. But in 2000 it got hip to design, commissioning Swai to create furnishings that could launch its new brand Hygge into high-end showrooms. The use of rubberwood, known locally as parawood, makes it more affordable than most premium furniture. The value is not in rare materials but in rarefied design.

This comes from the game Swai plays with style, as he turns design history into a chest full of toys. Alone among his Thai colleagues, he has pursued an eclectic, historicist approach a bit like the one pioneered in furniture designed in the 1980s by the American architects Michael Graves and Robert Venturi, not to mention Italy's Ettore Sottsass, founder of the renowned Memphis design group. These kindred designers, loosely grouped under the label postmodernist, flaunted modernist convention by dressing up their work in art-historical references and ornament. The excesses of postmodern style disenchanted design audiences in the 1990s, but Swai seems to have got it right. His wit is warm, not studied. He avoids the over-the-top decoration seen in the 1980s, finishing his furniture only in basic wood stains or lacquer in primary colours. Viewed alongside the earlier designers, Swai most resembles Venturi in his use of utility woods and planar forms. Just as Venturi delighted in quoting from sources spread over many centuries, Swai's collection invokes Ming-era chairs, early 20th-century avant-garde furniture and other period references that design fans will enjoy tracing. Some Swai

designs instead play with simile, metaphor or anthropomorphic form. Savvy work like this deserves wider notice than it has so far received.

Perhaps it has been overlooked because Swai himself is reclusive, shunning the media culture that, in Thailand more than elsewhere, turns artists and designers into celebrities better known for their faces in paparazzi shots than for their work. According to Swai's colleagues at Hygge, he has never spoken to a reporter, and he declined to be interviewed or photographed for this book. He graduated with a degree in graphic art from Silpakorn University in 1980, has worked in advertising, and in 2001 produced a book of his own computer graphic art compositions, *Somnambulist's Gallery*. In the preface to his book (quoted below), Swai explains his design philosophy, suggesting that he turned to international and historical influences to escape the confines of local tradition. This makes Swai a revisionist twice over, reinterpreting both local and global styles.

OPPOSITE: **PUPPET CHAIRS, 2004.** *Rubber tree wood.* Curved leg brackets and an anthropomorphic motif soften the rectilinear geometry of this chair.

BELOW LEFT: **BEETLE CHAIR, 2004.** *Rubber tree wood, lacquer finish.* This architectural design winks at Ming furniture and the steel chairs Frank Lloyd Wright created in 1936 for the Johnson Wax Building.

BELOW CENTRE: **PUZZLE CHAIR, 2004.** *Rubber tree wood, lacquer finish.* Swai's chair manages to be comfortable while recalling the geometric severity of avant garde classics like Gerrit Thomas Rietveld's 1934 Zig-Zag and 1918 Red and Blue.

BELOW RIGHT: **STUDIO CHAIR, 2004.** *Rubber tree wood.* A design that is as individual as it is simple.

"WE SHOULD NOT SIMPLY ADHERE TO THAINESS IN A STRICT SENSE, AND SHOULD AVOID THE KIND OF NARROW-MINDED ATTITUDES THAT MAKE US OBSESSED WITH NATIONALISM, TO THE POINT OF TASTELESSNESS... THE CONSERVATION OF THAINESS... HAS PLAYED A MAJOR ROLE IN THE ONGOING DECLINE OF OUR ARTISTIC AND CULTURAL IDENTITIES. IN MY WORK, I HAVE RELIED ON STUDIES OF MANY MASTERWORKS. I HAVE RESEARCHED IN MANY FIELDS OF KNOWLEDGE AND HAVE TRIED TO SORT THINGS OUT FOR MYSELF, AND DEVELOP GOOD TASTE..."

JITRIN JINTAPRECHA

LIVING FOR DESIGN A rising star among the third generation of Bangkok designers (those born in the 1970s), Jitrin Jintaprecha is one of the very few working as a consultant designer. A career as a freelance product designer barely existed in Thailand before 2001, the year Jitrin finished his bachelor's degree in industrial design. Had he graduated just a few years earlier, Jitrin might have had only two options: become a staff designer or start a company to produce his own designs. But the years since the late 1990s have seen the emergence of a number of local furniture brands that value design enough to commission new products, paying design fees and royalties.

OPPOSITE: **TARA CHAIR, 2005.** *Fibreglass.* Tara, meaning wave, is made with seven fibre-and-resin layers and can be used outdoors. Colour is integrated into the materials, not applied using paint, so scratches can be removed simply by polishing the surface. Redbox commissioned this design.

ABOVE: **KLING LOUNGE CHAIR, KLING JR. OTTOMAN, 2003.** *Steel-and-rubberwood frame, foam upholstery, fabric.* Jitrin wanted to design a rocking chair in upholstered form. The hollow space inside the chair, designed for Stone & Steel, can be used for storage of reading materials.

"I went to a desert in Arizona to observe the crawling of a snake that's capable of hopping short distances."

THAWAN DUCHANEE

PROMETHEAN Famous for his virtuoso drawing and painting since the 1960s, Thawan Duchanee has spent much of his time in recent decades working on a masterpiece of a different kind. Together with some 50 assistants, he has built Ban Dam—a compound in Chiang Rai province of some three dozen buildings, each one made according to his own innovative designs. There are houses, studios, workshops, dining halls, rock gardens and outdoor sculptures. The largest structure is a triple-roofed *viharn*, a timber hall larger than any wooden chapel in Thailand, which will house a collection of his most gigantic canvases. Several pavilions are purpose-built for such activities as bird-watching. An open-roofed plaster dome permits meditation while viewing the moon. Another dome hosts the farting festivals enjoyed by his hill tribe neighbours; its curving walls amplify sound.

OPPOSITE: **DESIRABLE AND UNDESIRABLE, 2003.** *Oil and gold leaf on canvas, 200 x 185 cm.* "Throughout our lives desire arises and then disappears, then arises again, never ending... I attempt to show the mystery of the natural instinct, its tremendous energy and strength."

Portrait photo by @nationphoto

"IN THE ARIZONA DESERT I SAW THE GOLDEN EAGLE, AND IN THE PHILIPPINES I TOOK THREE MONTHS TO OBSERVE THE BEHAVIOUR OF THE EAGLE THAT EATS MONKEY BRIANS ITS MOVEMENT IS SO FAST THAT THE MONKEY DOESN'T DETECT ITS EXISTENCE."

Conceived as a 'museum for mankind', a kind of open monastery for spiritual contemplation through art and nature, the compound likely surpasses any other artist's residence in the world in its ambition and artistry. For each unique building, Thawan has crafted his own sculptural furnishings, which also serve a ritualistic purpose.

Suggesting the totemic creations of a North American tribe, they are assembled from animal hides and bones that the artist has collected over a lifetime of world travel. Like the architecture, these furnishings are meant to convey a heightened sense of spiritual and aesthetic awareness, of connection to nature and the past.

Many of the artifacts served as models for his art, in which figures of animals play a central role as emblems of beauty, mystery and power. Often intertwined with his figures of humans and divinities, the creatures become metaphors for the human psyche and the artistic quest. Thawan, who also creates jewellery, decorative knives and axes, cites influences ranging from Salvador Dali to Michelangelo to tribal art. His architecture, too, is eclectic, melding ideas from Thailand, Burma, Laos, the Himalayas, Japan and Sumatra.

An art prodigy who held his first solo exhibition at the age of four, Thawan observed wild animals as a child in the forests of his home province of Chiang Rai, the mountainous extreme northern corner of Thailand, in the former opium-growing region known as the Golden Triangle. His father was a soldier who taught him to hunt. His mother, a traditional healer, took him into the jungle foraging for natural medicines. His fascination with animals continues: he keeps cobras and bobcats in several of his many homes.

BELOW AND OPPOSITE: **FURNISHINGS FROM BAN DAM.** Seating and beds from Thawan's Chiang Rai residence were exhibited at The Queen's Gallery in 2004. "I am a painter—I need something to sharpen my imagination. I have skulls, carcasses of carnivores, herbivores with single hooves or double hooves so that I can study their anatomy and use them for guidance. I need to see fangs, tusks, claws, talons, skin of carnivores because the senses of taste, touch, smell, sight and sound sharpen my imagination. Without these, my imagination cannot soar up to a supernatural state."

"My style is about lines and planes that intersect, shapes that interact, the play of light and shadow on lines of wood."

CHULAPHUN

CHULANOND
of Existenze

SQUARE NOT Sometimes even the most modern Bangkok designs contain hidden allusions to traditional Thai aesthetics. Chulaphun Chulanond's fine collection of wood furniture, for example, is rich in acute and oblique angles that hint at the geometry of old Siamese architecture. The elegant Siamese timber house abounds in trapezoids, with walls that taper inward toward the ceiling, mounted on posts that slant for increased stability. Chulaphun did not quote tradition consciously, but like local builders over the centuries, he shows an attraction to shapes having this kind of flair. His approach is contemporary, but using his own sense of form. "What he is trying to do is break the square format that everyone else uses," explains Veeraporn Nitiprapa, the jewellery designer who is his wife and collaborator in his brand, Existenze.

OPPOSITE: **FAST FORWARD 90 DINING CHAIRS, 2002.** *Solid oak.*

ABOVE: **SUNDAY'S SUNSET DECK CHAIR AND X TABLE, 2001.** *Plantation teak, leather/vinyl.*

"I'm really still like a child. I just want to play all day. Being a designer lets me do it."

PREEDA
SIRIPORNSUB

for Mobilia

A SENSE OF PLAY Preeda Siripornsub says he feels as if he has been training to become a designer all his life. His love of arts and crafts began in his early childhood, when he would spend time with his sister and the rest of his family drawing, painting, sculpting, doing origami and making paper flowers. Designing furnishings and interiors is a fulfillment of those early passions. "I'm really still like a child. I just want to play all day. Being a designer lets me do it," Preeda smiles.

In art college, he learned the intricacies of Thai classical arts like gold-and-lacquer painting and mural painting before studying interior design at Silpakorn University. From 2002 to 2004, he created three furniture collections for a new brand called Mobilia, a modern design line launched by a traditional furniture manufacturer established in 1980.

Preeda's 50 Mobilia designs include sofas, armchairs, tables and cabinets in many different configurations but with a consistent warmth and sense of play. This friendly mood comes from the use of colour, fabric, wood trim and gentle curves. The seating designs are very comfortable, thanks to ample cushioning

and big dimensions that encourage relaxation. Following both the brief given to him by Mobilia and Preeda's own predilections, most of the furniture shows a mix of contemporary Western style with abstracted Eastern references.

Many of the playful designs are based on Preeda's love of animals, cartoons, Disney movies and children's stories. His favourite design, for example, is his Flipper rocking chair (page 72), whose curved, wedge-like shape was inspired by the form of a swimming dolphin. Since the age of five, Preeda has loved dolphins, collecting dolphin toys and cartoons, watching them in National Geographic documentaries and in movies like *Flipper*. When he set out to design a rocking chair, the sea mammal's shape came to mind. "I love the dolphin's form, the way it moves in the sea. It's a lovely and friendly animal. So when I look at this chair I just feel happy. It's so fun and *sabai*, very relaxing."

The Muchoo chair (page 73) is an example of Preeda's East-West designs, named after the dragon in the Disney movie *Mulan*, which is based on a Chinese legend. The chair's form quotes a cloud motif used in traditional Chinese art and design, an abstract, geometric line that suggests the swirling vortex of a cloud. Preeda associates clouds with the heroes in Chinese legends who fly through the sky. He has loved these stories since childhood, all the more so because his ancestors came from southern China.

Preeda's decision to work with furniture came easily. His father is a contractor specialising in built-in furniture and cabinetry. This accounts for Preeda's close attention to quality control. He visits his factory every day to inspect each item before shipping. He knows a lot about wood, and tends to use sustainable sources in his designs: frames from the wood of durian trees, harvested from old fruit plantations. He uses plantation teak in the form of trim and veneer on plywood.

The designs shown here are from Preeda's work for Mobilia. Now he has founded his own firm, Innia, specialising in interior design, furniture and accessories, with an emphasis on handicraft. "I think craft is the future of design. Nowadays you see a lot of design products that are either completely handcrafted or else totally mass produced. I want to make products that mix both methods in equal balance."

OPPOSITE: **INKA ARMCHAIR, 2004**. *Plantation rubber wood inner frame, no-sag springs, polyester fabric, plantation teak armrest, stainless steel legs.* Inspired by a lecture-hall desk, the chair has a flippable armrest.

OPPOSITE: **SIDE TABLE, 2004.** *Laminated glass and stainless steel.*

ABOVE: **VERA ARMCHAIR, 2004.** *Plywood frame, plantation teak veneer, polyester foam cushions, stainless steel legs.* The structure is inspired by a basic form used in origami, one of Preeda's favourite handicrafts.

RIGHT: **SEXY'S ARMCHAIR, 2004.** *Plantation rubber wood inner frame, polyester foam, plantation teak armrest, stainless steel legs.* The 'S' shape of the armrest is inspired by the curved cloud motif used in Chinese decoration.

"My concept was to recycle old wood, so people would not have to cut down trees... I shaped my designs according to the materials at hand, not by finding material for the designs."

SAIYART SEMANGERN

POETRY IN WOOD Thailand has an important tradition of self-taught masters of painting, literature, music and other arts. Only one of these masters, however, has specialised in the creation of art furniture. Saiyart Semangern is a type of artist who is especially Thai, as conveyed by the poetry in his designs, their evocation of local craft and culture. Thainess also shows in the arc of his career, in his feisty independence and entrepreneurialism. There is a spiritual resonance in his work, but it seems less Buddhist than animist in its passion and mystery.

RIGHT: **THE FOREST CHAIR, 1992.** *Reclaimed timber yokes and other farm tools.* Saiyart's rustic early designs inspired a nationwide cottage industry of other craftsmen.

"I don't worry about whether I am rich or poor. Rich people have money, but I have ideas."

LEFT: **DOUBLE POWER, 2002.** *Reclaimed pulleys.* Saiyart is even more passionate about creating sculpture than making furniture.

OPPOSITE: **FARMER'S COFFEE SET TABLE AND CHAIRS, 2002.** *Steel, wood, glass.* Saiyart's 'found' designs show a rustic wit.

Ranging from rustic to refined, Saiyart's one-off designs are usually sculptural and full of *sanook*. Often they play with figure and use curvilinear form in seeming defiance of wood's rigidity. Many pieces emphasise the reclaimed materials from which they are made. The Forest chair (page 77) for example, is sculpted from old water buffalo yokes, which were traditionally made not by carving wood, but by training the branch of a live tree into the desired shape. Using long wires staked to the ground, this bonsai-like method gave the yoke great strength, a scrap of folk wisdom commemorated in Saiyart's design.

Born in the ancient capital of Ayutthaya, Saiyart became interested in carpentry as a child, when his father forced him to repair a verandah balustrade he'd broken on his family's old teak Siamese house. He studied construction at vocational school, worked

"A DOCTOR LIKED ONE OF MY TABLES AND OFFERED ME HALF PRICE.
I SAID, 'OK, LET ME CUT OFF TWO OF THE LEGS.' YOU CANNOT BARGAIN FOR
MEDICINE. THE SAME GOES FOR MY FURNITURE."

as a foreman, and during the 1970s did a stint in the Middle East installing custom furnishings for the big Italian firm, Castelli. When he returned to work in Thailand, he devoted his free time to his passion for arts and crafts, which he studied on trips upcountry or in Cambodia and Laos. He saved money for five years to be able to spend a month in the Australian outback studying aboriginal art and culture, eating grubs and kangaroo alongside his local hosts.

Duly inspired, he started making sculpture and furniture in 1984, using old wood reclaimed from buffalo carts, plows and rice barges. As rural Thais abandoned these venerable handmade tools in favour of power machinery or jobs in the city, Saiyart devised his own techniques and tools to make optimal use of the timber, which was otherwise scarce due to a ban on logging in Thailand's overexploited forests.

"My concept was to recycle old wood, so people would not have to cut down trees... I shaped my designs according to the materials at hand, not by finding material for the designs." Saiyart has exhibited his work in Bangkok hotels, selling out each time. Proof of the appeal of his work is the cottage industry of emulators it inspired. Nowadays it is hard to drive more than a few kilometres down any suburban road without seeing a yard or shop sporting at least one piece of folk furniture made from old wood in the Saiyart fashion. This work is charming in its own right, but rarely as strong as Saiyart's own designs, which he has taken to branding with a logo: "Saiyart: Carpenter & Artist." Saiyart says it has not been easy supporting his wife and children as an artisan, but he has been rewarded with exhibitions in the Netherlands and the United Arab Emirates, and did an acclaimed collaboration with leading architect Nithi Sthapitanonda in 2002 (page 18).

SORIES

ACCESSORIES ┃ML Pawinee Santisiri ┃Sakul Intakul ┃Gilles Caffier
┃Angus Hutcheson ┃Thaiwijit Poengkasemsomboon

ML PAWINEE SANTISIRI
of Ayodhya

DREAM WEAVER Water hyacinth is handsome when used in furniture, but it becomes simply beautiful in the accessories designed by ML Pawinee Santisiri. An interior designer schooled at Silpakorn University, ML Pawinee is the talent who pioneered the use of this natural fibre in contemporary crafts (see *Water Hyacinth*, page 210), first at a rural development research project from 1985 to 1987, and later at the group of firms she helped found, which includes Yothaka. At her own brand within the group, Ayodhya, she has innovated hundreds of designs for vases, trays, frames, baskets, lamps, mats and cushions. With their freshness and uncomplicated elegance, the best of these appear likely to stand as Bangkok classics.

What enables ML Pawinee to create so many designs from this single material is her mastery of woven construction. She developed more than a dozen weaving, braiding and other methods, each with a different look and

OPPOSITE: **FRINGE WEAVE (DETAIL).** *Sun-dried water hyacinth stems on wire mesh.* Cropped fibres create a porous, matte surface. This technique is used in the vessel shown in the Introduction (page 10).

ABOVE: **VARIOUS DESIGNS.** *Sun-dried water hyacinth stems on wire or wood bases.* Four Ayodhya designs show a variety of weaves (from left): wrap and bunch; braid; coil; and waffle techniques.

range of applications. Her 'fringe' weave, for example, creates a dense, matte surface. Water hyacinth stems are tightly woven onto a mesh of humble chicken-wire, then sheared for an unusual, brush-cut effect (page 84).

The same technique is reversed in her 'waffle' weave, which exposes the side where the stems are attached to the mesh. Other methods mix the fibre with materials like jute, leather and beads. She forms geometric designs by coiling the stems into squares. Tall baskets use a simple 'wrap' or 'bunch' weave on a wire frame, while a 'net' weave suits cushion covers.

Water hyacinth's light weight and flexibility lets ML Pawinee make even large vessels standing more than one and a half metres tall, in graceful shapes recalling classic Asian ceramics. Her application of this new material to the antique shapes highlights the fibre's contrast to pottery: its lightness, organic warmth and grassy fragrance. These are qualities that warm up modern interiors cooled by stone, steel and glass. With their understated aesthetic, Ayodhya designs are esteemed in Japan, where they have won awards and been exhibited at Tokyo's Hara Museum.

ML Pawinee is driven to innovate by the need to create two new collections each year that take advantage of the specific handicraft skills of her firm's more than 100 artisans, primarily using water hyacinth. She says her commitment to sustaining this village-size collective means that she would never consider mechanical production, outsourcing or a shift toward the mass market. The designs have to suit sophisticated interiors. They also should be difficult for copycats to imitate. "I feel bound to this material so I keep finding new ways to use it, to take it as far as it will go," says ML Pawinee, who despite her elite Bangkok background prefers rustic crafts to fancy luxury goods.

More than any other designer, ML Pawinee has worked not just for her own success, but to transform Bangkok design into a collective movement, through her mentoring and organisational talents. Daughter of an air marshal and a national bridge champion, she founded the Design & Objects Association in 1999 to raise the profile of Thai design in government-organised trade exhibitions, where high-end products had previously been displayed side-by-side with mass-market wares. The group enforces rules against copycats and rallies its members to require fair terms from buyers. In 2004, she organised an unprecedented exhibition and charity auction of classical Thai handicrafts to celebrate the 72nd birthday of Her Majesty Queen Sirikit. She also chaired the steering committee for the Thailand Creative and Design Center, opened to world acclaim in 2005.

"Thai people are humble in many ways. We don't talk big. We try to be harmonious and help each other. In our design association, we always think of the impact of creating things together instead of just individual showmanship. If other designers come to my company with their own designs, we'll produce for them. We are happy helping each other."

"I FEEL BOUND TO THIS MATERIAL SO I KEEP FINDING NEW WAYS TO USE IT, TO TAKE IT AS FAR AS IT WILL GO."

OPPOSITE: **VESSELS, 2005.** *Sun-dried water hyacinth stems using 'wrap' weave, wire frame.* These large vases combine classical, rustic and modern influences. The forms evoke the high art of ancient Khmer ceramics but the materials suggest village crafts. Such combinations show ML Pawinee's eclectic, contemporary sensibility. (The screen is a painting done in the traditional style of north-eastern Thai temple murals.)

FAR LEFT: **CORN FLOWER VESSEL, 2004.** *Porcelain.* The shape of a kernel of corn suggested this design.

LEFT: **TAMARINE FLOWER VESSEL, 2004.** *Porcelain.* This bud vase was inspired by the fruit of the tamarind tree.

BELOW: **MACLURA FLOWER VESSEL, 2004.** *Porcelain.* Sakul based this design on the globular form of the densely packed flowers of the Maclura fruticosa tree, which grows in northern Thailand.

OPPOSITE: **FLOWER VESSEL, 2004.** *Porcelain.* Perching on the edge of a shelf, this vase was inspired by the bulb of the crinum lily.

SAKUL INTAKUL

CUBE/SPHERE Throughout Sakul Intakul's design oeuvre—which ranges from floral installations to decorative accessories—there is a tone of rationality and deliberateness that hints at his background in engineering. He likes systems and forms, often relying on a framework of squares or cubes to help define his work. This geometry becomes a grid within which he improvises a design's details, its curves and movement. True to an engineer's purposiveness, his designs tend to solve problems, being economical, 'green' and easy to use.

His style might appear more Japanese or Chinese than Thai—and Sakul has studied ikebana after all—but the psychology of his work comports with the detached, rational attitude of South-east Asia's conservative form of Buddhism, Theravada, which is a philosophy of cultivated dispassion. Sakul's approach is also Thai in its delicacy and reliance on craft.

"I do a lot of preparation when I work—reading, travelling, talking to people, digesting new information. When it comes time to design, I feel very

safe. I stand on stable ground," says Sakul, who works closely with both clients and the people producing his designs—florists, metalsmiths and ceramicists.

His method is illustrated in his signature flower vessels. These delicate crafts are based on the forms of nuts, fruits and seeds native to Thailand. Sakul abstracts and refines the original forms before rendering them in porcelain or bronze. The resulting vessels act as quiet backdrops for individual blooms. This approach suits the extravagant forms of so many tropical flowers, which can be appreciated in isolation even more easily than in bouquets. The composition of flower and vase promotes a meditative focus. Or the vases can be displayed on their own, for their fine sculptural form.

Like the small vessels, Sakul's floral installations at Bangkok's Sukhothai Hotel and Conrad Hotel are naturally 'green' designs because the flowers only need to be replaced twice a week, creating less refuse than a typical bouquet-style approach. The arrangement is simple enough to be done by hotel staff instead of florists, saving cost.

Sakul's methodical approach enables him to innovate a steady progression of designs within each category that he explores, with consistently high quality. Likewise, this focus on concepts helps him try an ever-widening range of categories. The bud vases inspired a line of silver jewellery, and he has created candle stands, fragrances, potpourri, a stage design and gardens.

"I DO A LOT OF PREPARATION WHEN I WORK—READING, TRAVELLING, TALKING TO PEOPLE, DIGESTING NEW INFORMATION. WHEN IT COMES TIME TO DESIGN, I FEEL VERY SAFE. I STAND ON STABLE GROUND."

ABOVE: **FLOWER VESSELS, 2002.** *Bronze.* Plant seeds and seed pods inspired these small bud vases: (from left) Sea Pod, Trion, Twisted Pod.

OPPOSITE: **PONG PONG FLOWER VESSEL, 2002.** *Bronze.* Sakul casts the form of a Pong Pong tree seed in metal here.

90

GILLES CAFFIER

BELOW: **CURTAIN, 2001.** *Handmade ceramic beads on nylon filament.* The subtly random pattern in which the beads are strung conveys the design's manual construction.

SECRET QUALITIES Dark sensuality suffuses the designs of Gilles Caffier, a Frenchman who melds Asian-influenced minimalism with his own metropolitan chic in accessories like vases, candleholders, lamps and cushions. Some foreign designers come to South-east Asia to exploit luxury materials, often unsustainable ones, but Caffier relies on design innovation, crafting subtle textures, finishes and forms especially when using such ordinary materials as terracotta, acrylic, steel and mango tree wood. "I like to respect the materials, to use their secret qualities, but to make them disappear into a new thing," he says.

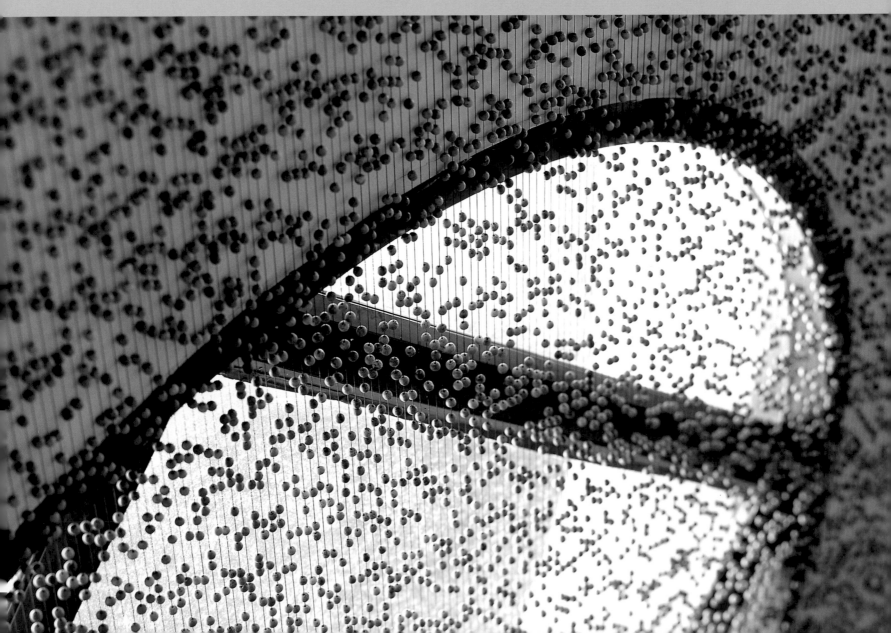

Caffier's strength is his signature style and perfectionist approach to construction. His best designs are as finely crafted as jewellery, like the bead curtains he produces from handmade leather disks and clay. When an interior designer ordered this product for a client's project, a team of ten of Caffier's artisans spent two months making the 600,000 components. Caffier discovered other customers were buying these same curtains to disassemble and sell as fashion jewellery.

A design multi-talent who previously worked in fashion, textiles and interiors, Caffier has spent most of his life in Asia, first in Tokyo, and since 1993 in Bangkok, where his workshop employs some 60 craftspeople. The Gilles Caffier Collection spans some 1,000 designs, many of them featured in the international media. They are sold through elite shops like Joseph and B&B Italia in London, and Neiman Marcus in the United States.

Obsessed by work, Caffier goes years at a time without vacationing. His products are difficult to design as well as to craft; developing a new model can take months of experimentation with prototypes and trial production runs. One example is a marble vessel that can be used for buds or to accommodate a floating candle. The vase takes the form of a wheel with a deep groove inside. Producing this particular shape requires the skills of an experienced craftsman able to carve the stone without shattering it. Even after much practice, the craftsman has to discard many efforts.

The beauty of such designs is deceptive in its simplicity, given how much craft they embody. A famous English buyer learned this when he visited Caffier's booth at a trade exhibition to source products for a large retail group. Caffier's Pineapple ceramic vase caught the Englishman's eye, so he asked how soon he could get 2,500 of them. Caffier had to reach for his calculator to answer: five-and-a-half years.

ANGUS HUTCHESON
of Ango

NATURAL BALANCE No Bangkok designer is more adventurous in using new materials than Angus Hutcheson, an English architect who moved to Thailand and started making lamps in 2002. His lighting designs are likely the first ever to use palm leaves, raw silk cocoons, shredded plantation timber, hand-moulded natural rubber and other unusual local materials, which he employs as the lamp diffuser, the exterior element of the fixture that refracts and distributes light from the bulb inside.

Hutcheson favours unmistakably natural materials that are renewable and can be used in raw or lightly processed form, so they consume less energy in production. He combines these organics with machined elements like stainless steel cantilevers. In this way, he means Ango designs to be sustainable in both technique and the message they convey. "It's a kind of allegory about how we can live alongside nature in a technological world."

Many Ango designs take a natural form as a starting point: a bird's nest, a chrysalis, a fish. They show a sense of proportion and structure that reflects Hutcheson's two decades of practicing architecture in England, the United States and Latin America. "The old truths of architecture—

OPPOSITE: **NATIVE TABLE LIGHT, 2003.** *Talipot palm leaf, hand-finished stainless steel base.* "The tripod base is an archetypal form, while the diffuser is like something an electro native would produce."

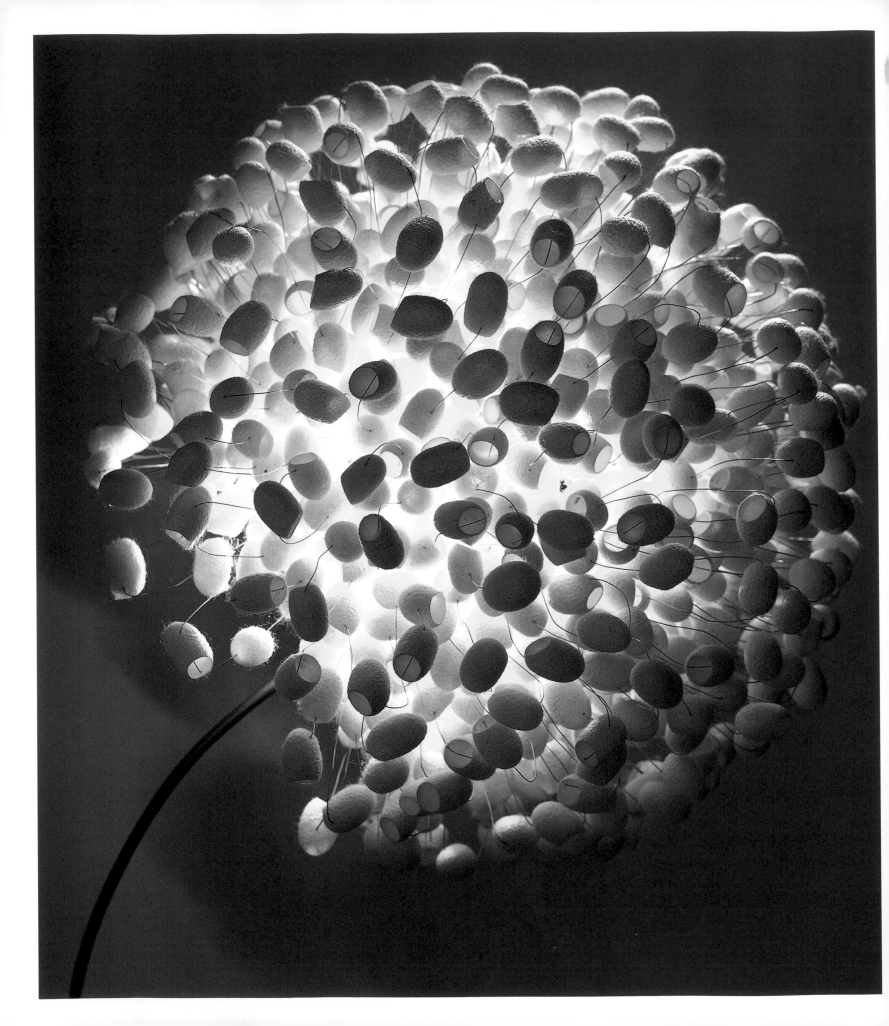

OPPOSITE: **CHRYSALIS SKY FLOOR LIGHT (DETAIL), 2003.** *Silk cocoons, stainless steel base.* This surreal design has become Ango's signature piece. The diffuser comprises a halo of hundreds of sun-bleached silk cocoons suspended in a soldered wire matrix.

ABOVE: **SILK AURA FLOOR LIGHT, 2003.** *Raw silk, stainless steel base.* "This design was conceived as an oval form on the most delicate cantilevered structure we could invent. The diffuser is the culmination of our experimenting with silk in its natural state with serecin intact."

BELOW: **NEST TABLE LIGHT, 2003.** *Rattan, stainless steel base.* The random circular form of the diffuser is attained using specially extruded ratttan.

honourable intention, delight, usefulness—hold fast in furniture and lighting as well. In designing a lamp, form and structure are both vital, as they are in architecture, but materials become more important—their texture, colour rendering and light diffusion."

Hutcheson's work is kindred to that of his friends Udom Udomsrianan, ML Pawinee Santisiri and Suwan Kongkhunthian, who have exhibited together with him at Tokyo's Hara Museum. His approach recalls the biomorphic furniture and lighting designs of mid-century modern figures like American sculptor Isamu Noguchi, but showing a bolder experimentation with materials and form. Hutcheson's success in giving such strong aesthetic expression to design with sustainable characteristics points toward a promising new direction for applied arts in Thailand. "What's happening in design here is not just a shift in fashion, but people now looking at the bigger picture—ecology and how we use resources. It's not just muesli sustainability. It has to be sophisticated for consumers today."

"It's a kind of allegory about how we can live alongside nature in a technological world."

THAIWIJIT POENGKASEMSOMBOON

ALCHEMY An artist known for his industry and professionalism, Thaiwijit Poengkasemsomboon possesses a creativity that spans many categories. As an art student in Bangkok and Poland, he trained in printmaking, but later made his mark as one of Thailand's leading abstract painters, known for canvases that buzz with jazzy energy and colour. He has adapted his improvisationalist aesthetic to sculpture and one-off design objects like lamps, furniture, interior fixtures and pots. At times he orchestrates all these elements at once to compose interiors and architectural designs for spaces like restaurants and hotels (see *Reflections Rooms*, pages 162–163).

Thaiwijit's design objects are mostly resurrected from junked machinery, reclaimed furniture components and discarded construction materials. Usually he combines these elements with pipe, cement, electrical fittings or other generic materials bought from the hardware store. The resulting designs are alive with quirky personality. The creative process of recycling doubles the pleasure for the artist: he delights both in making things, and in

BELOW: **BOOKWORM TABLE LAMP, 2002.** *Tubular steel chair parts, car engine air filter, metal float from water tank, metal wheels, cast aluminium electrical junction box, cast cement, halogen bulb.*

discovering their raw ingredients, often in junkyards or second-hand markets. For him, rapture might mean finding an old oil drum with an especially raw surface texture and unusual mouldings.

The designs hint at the personality of their protean creator, who is optimistic, good-humoured, independent, entrepreneurial and, in all this, really Thai. He credits his resourcefulness to his upbringing as one of eight children of a noodle-shop owner in the deep-south province of Pattani. "I had to develop many different abilities to help run my parents' restaurant. Thanks to this I know how to deal with things."

Like his personality, Thaiwijit's aesthetics are rather Thai, but they upend traditional Thai style. Conventional Thai aesthetics—as expressed in textiles, palace crafts and classical architecture—call for symmetry, harmony, fine pattern and detail, true colours and prettiness. In contrast, Thaiwijit's shapes are oblong, his proportions asymmetrical. His colours are often the neutral tones of raw plywood, cement and unfinished metal. Other times he uses paint in offbeat industrial hues: fluorescent orange, powder green, grey-purple.

The Thainess of all this lies in the artist's genius for transposition. His work conveys both the primitive, folkish sensibility of rural crafts and the gritty, densely layered textures and imagery of Thailand's endearingly ramshackle urban environment. It's not just that you can sense Bangkok in his work. It's that you begin to see Thaiwijit in the Bangkok all around: the storefronts with their layers of paint, handmade signage, gates and wires; the colourful trucks decorated by their drivers; the maze of impromptu construction. In this, his functional objects transcend the usual boundaries of design, and reveal themselves as works of real art.

"I had to develop many different abilities to help run my parents' restaurant. Thanks to this I know how to deal with things."

OPPOSITE: **FRUIT FLOOR LAMP, 2003.** *Reclaimed metal drum, light bulbs, metal pipe, cast cement base, refrigeration compressor casing, curtain rollers.* The diffuser is made of spent lamps used for night-time squid fishing in the artist's native province of Pattani. An outboard dimmer switch is mounted in its own moveable unit made from half a cast-iron fuselage for a refrigeration compressor. Curtain rollers serve as wheels.

CENTRE: **'A' CHAIR, 2002.** *Auto exhaust pipes, steel mesh.* The design is asymmetrical but comfortable, thanks to its ample seat.

THIS PAGE: **BUOYANT BUG LAMP, 2003.** *Cast aluminium body reclaimed from medical scale, eye bolt, wire mesh, wheels, tungsten bulbs.* Wheels and a handle allow this design to be used as floor, table or hanging lamp.

"My intent is to give value to worthless objects by recycling them or changing their original function into something new."

POP & KITSCH | **Vipoo Srivilasa** | **Anusorn Ngernyuang** | **Anurak Suchat** | **Chaiyut Plypetch** | **Satit Kalawantavanich**

TOP RIGHT: **MERMAID'S PET TEA SET, 2000.** *Earthenware*. A teapot, sugar bowl, milk jug and cup romancing Australia's coral reefs. (Photo by Michael Kluvanek, courtesy of Über Gallery, Melbourne)

TOP LEFT: **MERMAID'S PET TEA POT, 2000.** *Earthenware*. Some Vipoo works can be read as affectionate reflections upon the perky Aussie personality. (Photo by Michael Kluvanek, courtesy of Über Gallery, Melbourne)

LEFT: **YELLOW CORAL VASE, 2004.** *Earthenware*. Living by the sea in Tasmania inspired Vipoo to craft vessels like this. (Photo by the artist, courtesy of Über Gallery, Melbourne)

Portrait photo of Vipoo by Dean Netherton

VIPOO SRIVILASA

FABLES IN CLAY Teapots as polychrome, googly-eyed sea monsters. The Neo-Rococo ceramic statuette of a bodybuilder lifting gilded dumbells, wearing a golden blindfold. Funky blue-and-white vessels created for Bangkok collectors but satirising urban Thai obsessions with wealth, status and luxury goods.

Ceramics become *sanook* in the hands of Vipoo Srivilasa, a Melbourne-based artist who revels in subverting arch-bourgeois genres like 18th-century English porcelain figurines. Vipoo has kilned a memoir in clay of his impressions and dreams, a personal narrative that ranges in tone from sweetly ironic to campy to surreal. Australian life inspires the Bangkok expatriate with its strange flora and fauna, the spectacle of Sydney's Mardi Gras, even the crass imagery printed in junk mail. From Thailand, he brings forms and motifs he knows from traditional ceramics, costume and architecture, as well as puppetry and literature.

Vipoo has a technical mastery that shows 14 years of full-time studies in art from the age of 15. After finishing a bachelor's degree in ceramics at Bangkok's Rangsit University in 1994, he moved to Melbourne for a postgraduate ceramics course at Monash University, then to Hobart in 1998 for a master's programme in ceramics at the University of Tasmania. Life in seaside Hobart inspired Vipoo's many collections exploring marine creatures. Textured using press-moulds created from specimens like starfish and shells,

LEFT: **GOLDEN BOY, 2001.** *Earthenware.* Vipoo potrays the bodybuilder's quest as deluded. (Photo by Terence Bogue, courtesy of Über Gallery, Melbourne)

OPPOSITE: **HOPE BOWL, 2004.** *Cool Ice porcelain.* A neo-blue-and-white set of rice bowls tweaks Bangkok's love of luxury. (Photo by Terence Bogue, courtesy of Surapon Gallery, Bangkok)

each vessel received as many as five firings, with multiple layers of glossy and matte glazes. Faux diamonds and pearls stud the surfaces, a legacy of Vipoo's Bangkok undergraduate days working part-time as a jewellery designer. These aquatic fantasies led to two series of tea sets crafted as imaginary monsters.

Another ocean theme is mermaids, a Vipoo obsession. The artist dates this odd fascination to childhood, when his grandmother read him tales from the *Ramakien*, the Thai version of India's ancient *Ramayana* epic. He was particularly drawn to the character of Supan Madcha, a mermaid caught between the forces of good and evil. Vipoo has since come to see this character as an emblem of his own existence caught between two cultures—West and East, Australia and Thailand, gay and straight. Vipoo's undergraduate thesis was a collection of ceramic mermaids in cabaret-style drag, whom he was later astonished to discover in the flesh during his first visit to Sydney's flamboyant Mardi Gras bacchanal. On many a parade float there, Vipoo saw the demure sea dwellers of myth enthroned as creatures of outrageous majesty. These personae inspired his S&M Mermaid figurines (2000), cheeky self-portraits in which the artist imagined himself in submission to a fin-tailed, elaborately coiffed dominatrix. Vipoo intended these works as a tweak at repressive attitudes toward homosexuals within Thai society (page 11).

Still more philosophical yet just as fun are works parodying the vanity and conspicuous consumption that Vipoo observes in both Australia and urban Thailand. Inspired by the twee vignettes of domestic and pastoral life portrayed in antique Chelsea figurines, Vipoo created his Action Man series of bodybuilders (2001, 2002), a wry look at the self-absorption of gym addicts. His first Bangkok exhibition, *Lai Krarm* (2005), featured a collection of neo-blue-and-white vessels lampooning consumerism. Each piece depicts the objects of modern Thai desire: cosmetics, jewellery, luxury cars. Traditional auspicious fish motifs are rendered with scales shaped like Louis Vuitton logos. Vipoo signals a Buddhist awareness of evanescence by juxtaposing these images with memento mori like skulls and skeletal hands. One blue-and-white figure shows a woman pulling her face taut with her fingers as she envisions the effects of a face-lift. Beyond Vipoo's poke at vanity, the image suggests a wry reference to his technique of shaping ceramics by finger, pinching the clay into shape, or coiling and moulding it. He shuns the use of a potter's wheel, wanting a lively, hand-wrought look rather than smooth perfection. Vipoo says his work is influenced by such contemporary ceramicists as Adrian Saxe of the United States, Australia's Stephen Benwell, Thailand's Panchalee Sathirasas and his Rangsit University mentor Surojana Sethabutra. Not to mention his grandmother's mermaids.

ANUSORN
NGERNYUANG
of Reflections Thai

OPPOSITE: **REFLECTIONS THAI RETAIL SHOP.** At Bangkok's Suan Lum Night Bazaar, Anusorn's firm purveys what it calls "distinctive and smart 'musts' for the real individualistic identity".

A QUESTION OF TASTE To better savour the subversiveness of Anusorn Ngernyuang's designs, it's helpful to keep in mind the difference between kitsch style, his specialty, and kitsch itself. *Kitsch* is a German term coined by art theoreticians to refer to art and design that, from a sophisticated point of view, is maudlin, excessive or embarrassingly mediocre. Kitsch style is the campy, postmodern celebration of kitsch, half ironic, half sincere. From a rather condescending Western point of view, Asia has long been seen as a bountiful but unwitting source of kitschy stuff. And the region will probably continue to abound in kitsch, at least until the day consumers in Asia see

"Personally, I try to avoid kitsch. But I do keep a plastic flower in my room because it's so easy to care for."

eye-to-eye with Western arbiters of taste. Kitsch style, on the other hand, has been slow to catch on in places like Thailand. Its ironic attitude violates the taboo against ridicule. Style is taken at face value so that others don't lose face. (As when the style is found in places like your parents' living room, where kitsch tends to rule.)

Recently, however, a few Asian designers have become shameless purveyors of kitsch style. You can make fun of things and still be a good son, especially when you are, like Anusorn, the number one son of a horror novelist. "My parents knew I was strange," confesses the designer, whose descent into kitsch began in his teens, when he left home to study in Germany. He worked there in the hotel business before moving to Holland to open three successful Thai restaurants. Further success came upon befriending an Amsterdam neighbour, who happened to be renowned Czech designer Borek Sipek. He became a mentor to Anusorn, who after 20 years abroad returned to Bangkok to handle production of Sipek's furniture and houseware. Soon Anusorn launched his own collection, aptly described in the Reflections' product literature as "Trendy stuff to purify the modern home in a most advanced mode".

Kitsch wares have traditionally been mass-produced; Anusorn's twist is handcrafting them, like baskets and ottomans woven from a rainbow of PVC plastic instead of the natural materials village artisans normally use. "Even if something is not kitsch, you can turn it into kitsch, especially with colour. Kitsch hits you first with colour. You feel it deep inside your soul." With his sketchbook ever on hand, Anusorn has come up with thousands of designs for houseware

and accessories: rugs, baskets, furniture, lamps, handbags, luggage, figurines and more. It all sells voluminously in Europe's department stores and boutiques, giving Anusorn the last laugh on Western arbiters of taste.

And it's not only for export. Young Bangkokians are turning from ubiquitous kitsch toward the niche of kitsch style, which appeals to their sense of colour and *sanook*. It also appeals as an instant form of recycling; the wink of an eye turns bad taste into good.

Anusorn proved this decisively in 2004, when he converted a 1950s apartment block into a shrine of kitsch style, the Bangkok art hotel Reflections Rooms (page 158), an overnight hit. Ironically, though, Anusorn prefers to take his kitsch in small doses when not on the job. He's a sensitive type with an allergy to dust, so his own apartment is a shrine of minimalism: purified of little but a bed, television, reading lamp and single plastic flower.

OPPOSITE: **BOBB... BOBB... FOLDING CHAIRS, 2002.** *Cotton, PVC, fur, aluminium structure.* Utility seating gets an Anusorn makeover.

RIGHT: **MELON TALKS CHAIR.** *Wood frame, PVC.*

ANURAK SUCHAT
of Aesthetic Studio

TOP LEFT: **BEER LAMP, 2003.** *Laser-cut acrylic.* Anurak's Cocktail Collection of table lamps also features Wine and Brandy designs based on goblet forms.

TOP RIGHT: **'A' LAMP, 2003.** *Acrylic.* The inner and outer layers are moulded in different colours so that the lamp changes hues when the bulb inside is switched on.

OPPOSITE: **CROWN PENDANT LAMP, 2004.** *Polypropylene.*

PAGE 118, 119: **CONNEX WINE RACK, 2004.** *Anodised extruded aluminium.* Units can be combined in a variety of configurations, in any size ranging from a tabletop rack for six bottles to wall-size storage for an entire cellar.

TECH-FRIENDLY COOL Unpretentiously cool products for the young urbanite: that's the aesthetic of Anurak Suchat, who specialises in such accessories as lighting, tabletop items, desk tools and similar functional designs. Anurak is a gadget lover, so not surprisingly his products hint at technological inspiration, in materials ranging from laser-cut acrylic to anodised aluminium. But he transcends a flashy 'high-tech' look by using friendly colours and shapes, earning him many awards.

Anurak started out as a landscape architect, but shifted to designing products for export after the Thai economy's 1997 crash. The Chiang Mai native says his landscape work helped him think outside the box as a product designer. "It taught me to always consider the big picture because landscape design is the first stage in any architectural plan. When you have a plot of land, you have to analyse it, divide it up properly, plan infrastructure like roads, and have it all look beautiful as well. It combines function and aesthetics." This profession also gave Anurak skills in using computer tools like CAD-CAM. When he shifted from landscape design to product design, he utilised the same software and simply shrank the scale. But before rendering by computer, he thinks on paper. Anurak keeps a sketchbook by his bedstand

"I don't stick to any one material. I'm interested in form and function. If you have the right form, you can change the material to change the product's feeling."

at night, and on hand all day, the better to illustrate new inspirations the moment they come to mind. He finds some 300 ideas a year to be fed into the computer and transformed into potential products. Anurak handles CAD-CAM well enough to skip the product mock-up stage; he proceeds straight to production in most cases.

His favourite design is his Connex wine rack, available in nine metallic colours. He had surveyed the global design-scape and found only five or six strong examples in the product category of wine racks. Inspiration for his own offering came from some jigsaw puzzle toys he had bought in Hong Kong. He chose anodised extruded aluminium for its high strength, light weight, colour capability and recyclability. Precision was another consideration, since the rack units need to fit together snugly.

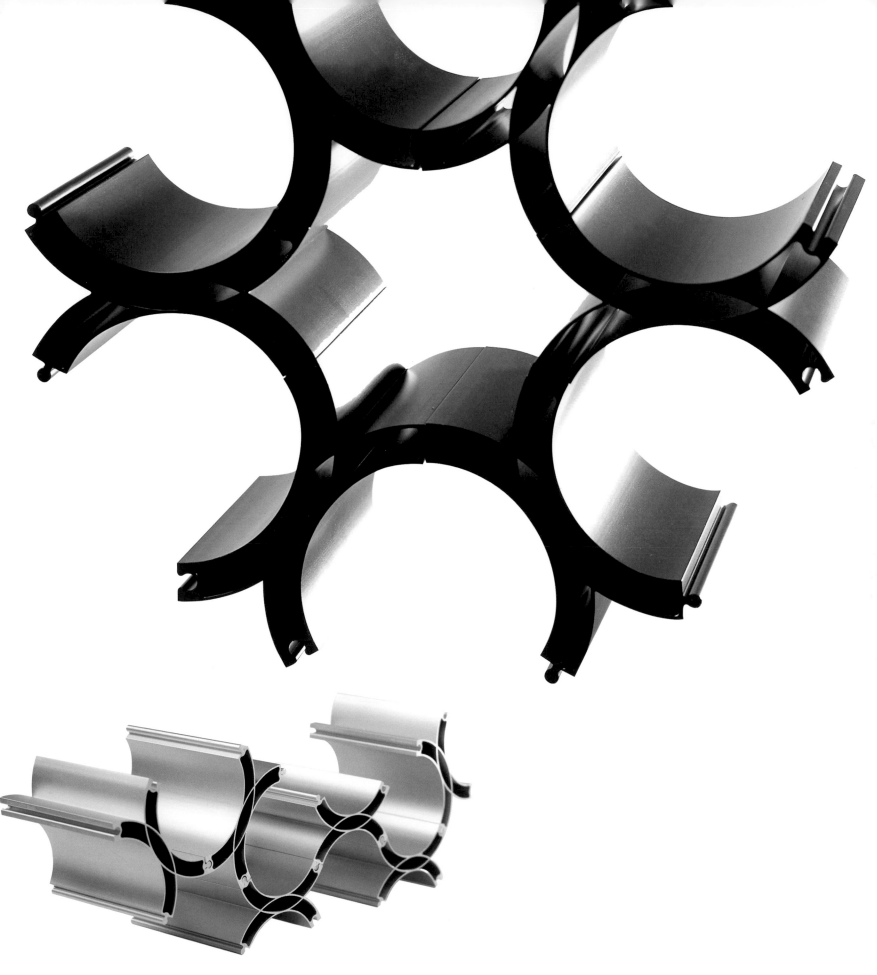

CHAIYUT PLYPETCH
of Propaganda

MR. P Customers in design boutiques and museum shops around the world fall in love with Propaganda products thinking they come from a design centre like Belgium or Helsinki. But a closer look at these gadgets reveals not a dry Northern wit but the spirit of *sanook*, the impish sense of fun that has won Thais a global reputation in endeavours like the creation of television commercials. Few know this better than Propaganda's co-founder Satit Kalawantavanich, who happens to be an advertising film director and president of a small Bangkok studio that in 2005 won the most awards of any ad production house in the world, beating big American and European rivals thanks mostly to works based on humour. Similarly, Propaganda, founded in 1994, has won Thailand's longest list of international product design awards.

THIS PAGE AND OPPOSITE:
MR. P COLLECTION, 2002–2004.
Chaiyut's iconic imp animates things like lamps, key-chains, ashtrays and coffee mugs. (Graphics and key-chain photo courtesy of Propagandist Co.)

Mascot of the firm is Mr. P, the droll naked boy who becomes such objects as doorstops, tape dispensers, key rings and candles. "Mr. P symbolises our profession as designers. Our work is our passion but it's also a kind of torture because it is so difficult," Satit says. "So Mr. P is the kind of person who sacrifices himself to be useful to other people. You pull tape from his mouth like pulling out his tongue, and you cut it off at his feet. Our job is to take an idea like this that's a little bit disgusting and turn it into a product. We don't make it ugly or cruel, but something lovely!"

In other products, Mr. P turns naughty, often peeing or farting. His creator, designer Chaiyut Plypetch, makes all this socially acceptable by crafting the mascot with a cartoonish lack of realistic detail. "If you put in fingers, toes, nipples it would be disgusting. This approach is more symbolic," Chaiyut observes. Mr. P was born from the designer's struggle to find a new idea for a lamp. When he started sketching an anthropomorphic design, he focused on the question of where to place the switch. "I knew it had to be at the middle of Mr. P's body, but not the belly button. It had

to stick out. I wanted to make it fun to use." Chaiyut describes himself as very *gep got*, bottled up, the kind of person who restrains his emotions, sometimes until they explode. Designing products like Mr. P became a way to express himself. Beyond this iconic character, Propaganda is also known for many household gadgets that show a cooler rendition of *sanook*—urbane but accessible. Examples include the Ap-Peel fruit bowl with a built-in knife, and the Tooth series of molar-shaped containers for toothpicks, tooth-brushes and candies (page 13).

"YOU SEE A LOT OF USEFUL THINGS AT A DEPARTMENT STORE, BUT YOU HAVE ALREADY USED THEM. WE TRY TO CREATE A NEW EXPERIENCE FOR THE USER, TO PLAY WITH DREAMS."

SATIT KALAWANTAVANICH
of Propaganda

"Form, function, materials are not enough—they lack life. The only way to make them come to life is using the dream of the designer."

TEXTILES | **TINNART NISALAK** | **JAKKAI SIRIBUTR** | **PLOENCHAN MOOK VINYARATN**
| **LAWANA POOPOKSAKUL** | **SASIWAN DUMRONGSIRI** | **JRUMCHAI SINGALAVANIJ**
| **WORRACHAI SIRIWIPANAN** | **MONTRI TOEMSOMBAT**

"Later I find myself looking at my watch, and suddenly I see the textile pattern was inspired by the dial, or by something like my shoes. Your mind records the things it likes, and eventually they become design."

TINNART NISALAK
of Jim Thompson

REPATRIATION Many Thai designers have benefited from having had a good mentor, but the one with the most renowned mentor of all is Tinnart Nisalak, a key Bangkok figure as senior home furnishing fabrics designer at The Thai Silk Company. After graduating with a degree in textile design from New York's Syracuse University in 1976, Tinnart had the coveted opportunity to join the Manhattan studio of Jack Lenor Larsen, one of the giants of modern textile design, where he worked for two years. By that time the textile scene was heating up in Thailand. Growing demand for Jim Thompson silk had outpaced capacity, so the company decided to build an upcountry weaving workshop, instead of only buying cloth from commissioned workers. Larsen, who had worked with Thompson in the 1950s and 1960s, saw this as a chance for Tinnart to apply his talents back home, so he recommended him to the firm. Tinnart joined the company in 1983, working alongside a fellow Larsen protégé, Gerald Pierce.

Tinnart says Larsen gave good advice on how to develop commercially as well as artistically successful designs. The American encouraged him to use his background in architecture to better conceptualise textiles (Larsen, Tinnart and Thompson all studied architecture as undergraduates). As a renowned art connoisseur, Larsen helped inspire Tinnart's own passion for collecting. In his office and Bangkok home, Tinnart displays materials for inspiration like

OPPOSITE: Tinnart designs brighten a collection of ottomans.

traditional baskets, antique ceramics, lacquer ware and ornamental plants. He also keeps pets like dogs, roosters and Siamese fighting fish.

Tinnart begins the design process by gathering images and found objects like leaves, then pinning them to a cork board to create a collage of colours, patterns and textures—the raw ingredients of imagination. He has created a huge variety of textiles as head of a large team responsible for two annual collections, each with up to 15 designs in as many as 30 colours, or some 600 different fabrics a year. Most show qualities of warmth, refinement and a rather Thai focus on detail. Tinnart is friendly, easy-going and optimistic, which is reflected in designs that are fresh and accessible. His textiles are innovative, but rarely radical. Like his mentor, Tinnart is attuned to end-users' tastes, and he designs to please.

OPPOSITE TOP: **LISU, 2003.** *Silk, handwoven with polyester.* Tinnart's designs reveal subtleties over time. Using thick and thin yarns, he layers texture and colour to build complex patterns.

OPPOSITE BOTTOM: **MADISON, 2001.** *Silk with cotton chenille.* Tinnart often achieves a sophisticated blurring of lines between tradition and modernity. This design uses textured yarns and patterning unusual for an ikat fabric.

BELOW: **LAHU, 2003.** *Silk.* This complex neo-traditional design puts ikat-dyed weft threads on a pattern-dyed warp background.

"DESIGNING TEXTILES IS A LOT LIKE COOKING. YOU PUT IN COLOURS IN THE RIGHT PROPORTIONS JUST LIKE USING SALT, PEPPER AND SPICE. I TAKE A BIG STRIPE OF RED, ADD A LITTLE LINE OF ORANGE AND SOME GREEN, ALL IN THE RIGHT BALANCE, EXCEPT THAT NO ONE ELSE CAN TELL YOU WHAT IS RIGHT. IT'S ALL YOUR OWN INTUITION."

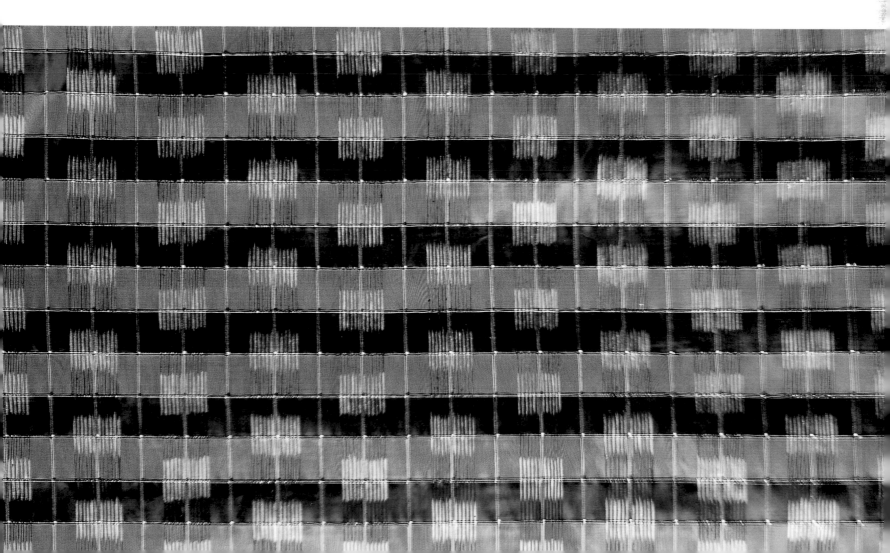

JAKKAI SIRIBUTR

ABSTRACT EXPRESSIONS Many of the best Bangkok furnishings and textiles are created by people who first trained as artists before going into design. But Jakkai Siributr did the reverse, studying commercial art before becoming a studio artist. While studying for his bachelor's and master's degrees in textile design in the United States, he devoted his free time to painting. After graduation, he found he had little passion to make products for the marketplace, so he turned to art. The results include these densely layered textile constructions, descendents of abstract expressionist painting but using fabric and thread.

Jakkai draws inspiration from both modern art and traditional crafts. He loves South-east Asian textiles, like those woven by Thailand's hill tribes, as well as the quilts crafted in Indiana and Pennsylvania, the American states where he studied, which are renowned centres for quilt-making. "You see these lines and stitches going all over the quilt. The handiwork gives it visual energy. I love all this folk art because you can see that the maker's hand and heart and mind went into crafting it."

In a similar way, Jakkai puts his own spirit and contemplation into his artworks, creating abstractions that can be seen as landscapes, vignettes of emotion, dreamy impressions of colour and pattern. He uses materials ranging from scraps of handwoven silk to the cheap floral prints he buys in Pahurat, a Bangkok Indian market famous for cloth. Working on the floor of his studio, Jakkai constructs his creations by taking the cloth and cutting or tearing it, then sewing it down in layers. Often he paints on top or embroiders it with

OPPOSITE: **DIURNAL, 2004.**
*Commercially printed Thai silk,
industrial cloth tape, plastic beads.
100 x 200 cm.*

THIS PAGE, FROM LEFT:
TRIP, 2004. *Hand-woven and
commercially printed Thai silk;
plastic beads; industrial cloth tape.
150 x 150 cm.*

RED HALLUCINATION, 2004.
*Commercially printed fabric, screen-
printed with pigment; hand-woven
Thai silk with mud and natural dyes;
industrial cloth tape. 150 x 150 cm.*

WITHIN, 2004. *Mud and natural dyes
on commercially printed Thai silk;
screen printed with pigment.
150 x 150 cm.*

QUELL, 2004. *Commercially printed
fabric and Thai silk; screen-printed
with pigment. 150 x 150 cm.*

materials like industrial tape and plastic beads. "It is mixed media, but I am staying true to textile traditions—techniques like hand sewing, quilting and using woven materials. I don't frame my work, but hang it, to retain this textile quality."

These works of fibre art are freely open to interpretation, but for the artist himself, they represent a therapeutic process of creation. "It's all about being in the present. It's my personal journal, reflecting my experiences and emotions through pattern, textures and colours. For example, as a Buddhist, I ask myself how does one follow the Five Precepts and go out in the world and work and encounter all kinds of people and problems. That is always going to be my quest in life, to find a way to do it. I may not be able to follow the Five Precepts all the time,

but I can at least be good enough to have a balanced life."

Jakkai often reflects on the rich social meanings in textiles. "Sometimes I use cheap, glittery fabric from Chinatown. It's made from polyester to replicate the exquisite, lacelike textiles that were once used in old Siam as court costume. At every government function today, you see people dressed in traditional costume, but it's really just this kitsch fabric you can buy for 25 baht a metre. It's also bought by people who work in cabarets and massage parlours, because it's golden and glittery. In villages upcountry, you see people wearing handwoven silk while working during the day, and then polyester from Korea when they go out at night. With that in mind, I like to mix things up, expensive and cheap, to make it into a piece of art."

RIGHT: **CHAOS, 2004.** *Commercially printed fabric and Thai silk, screen-printed with pigment. 100 x 200 cm.*

FAR RIGHT: **GLOW, 2004.** *Commercially printed fabric, Thai silk, synthetic dyes. 100 x 200 cm.*

OPPOSITE: **'A MANGO IS AN ORANGE', 2001.** *Silk, hemp, cotton. 120 x 125 cm. This early Jakkai work found a home in the dining room of publishing executive Gretchen Worth.*

"It's my personal journal, reflecting my experiences and emotions through pattern, texture and colour."

PLOENCHAN MOOK VINYARATN
of Beyond Living

NATURE'S TOUCH In the Bangkok of the 1980s, being very sophisticated often involved Western things—a US or UK education, English or French fluency, European travel, foreign fashions and furnishings. Ploenchan Vinyaratn, scion of a banking clan, had all those sophistications and more, but when she returned home in 1995 after long years of study in England, her fellow Thai creatives were starting to rediscover their own culture. By 1998, she found herself helping drive the collective process of innovation in her work as a designer. That was the year Ploenchan, known as Mook, joined Mae Fah Luang, the royal foundation helping hill tribes prosper through handicrafts. Having studied fashion textile design at London's Central St. Martin's College of Art and Design, she was well equipped to help give the group's hand-loomed textiles an international look better suited to the marketplace. She

ABOVE: **FROM BENEATH THE BLUE COLLECTION, 2004.** *Cotton, acrylic, gold and ultrasuede.* Markings of the Siamese Tigerfish inspired the cushion at left, while the design at right renders the layers of pattern and colour seen in clusters of coral.

PAGE 137: **CUSHION COVERS FROM BENEATH THE BLUE COLLECTION, 2004.** *Cotton, acrylic, gold and ultrasuede.* Mook riffs on Tigerfish patterns in many jazzy colours here.

"To do new things in textiles it's best to go deep and work from the inside out."

developed a characteristic style—earthy but alive—mixing diverse fibres, textures and colours. It showed contemporary flair but stayed rooted in the warm, highly textural qualities of hand-made cloth.

Mook took her style further in 2003, when she started her own brand, Beyond Living. Her designs became bolder, often using fashion textile techniques like quilting and embroidery. She built hand-looms five metres wide to produce very large rugs. Her graphics became more vibrant. "I'm a maximalist, not a minimalist. I like fun work—colourful things and lively things," she says. For Mook, liveliness and maximalist colour is best discovered in the world of nature, especially tropical nature. She builds collections around graphics inspired by living things like orchids, butterflies and creatures of the coral reef. "Design is already all around us. Things have already been designed! When I get inspired, I zoom in on things, then add to it and work on it to create a new thing. It's not copying, but you can trace where it came from. It has roots!"

The roots of Mook's style are eclectic. The patterns and graphics are European, but the spicy colours are local. Some of her designs weave iridescent chenille yarns together with rustic fibres like jute and banana bark sourced from upcountry markets and even non-woven materials like leather, vinyl or ultrasuede (pages 124–125). She knows her buyers well—high-end resorts, hotels and boutiques, interior designers like Bill Bensley—so she trusts her own design instincts more than the international colour forecasts. "I have a niche market—highly individual people. They are people who follow their emotions. Trends are for the big companies who want to play it safe."

LAWANA POOPOKSAKUL
of Mae Fah Luang

PAINTING IN THREADS She attended high school in the American state of Connecticut, and studied art and textiles at Rhode Island School of Design, but after repatriating to Thailand in 2001 Lawana Poopoksakul realised that idyllic New England could hardly inspire in the same way as Bangkok. The city's happy chaos helped her develop modern approaches to local textile identity. "Thai design doesn't have to come from the ornamentation of temples and palaces. It can be about the funny cartoons and the bad soap operas, or the way people go out in the streets in Bangkok in the evening wearing their pajamas, or the ladies doing aerobics in front of the Tesco store."

Lawana worked exclusively with handwoven textiles from 2001 to 2005, succeeding Ploenchan Vinyaratn as lead designer at Mae Fah Luang, the royal foundation supporting hill tribe communities through premium handicrafts (see *Princess from the Sky*, page 206). Among her collections there was

HANG TAO COLLECTION, 2004. *Cotton.* Graphics suggested by the everyday imagery of Bangkok storefronts became this handmade design. Lawana did the architectural snapshots on this page to use for inspiration.

her Hang Tao (Shophouse) series, 2004, inspired by the facades of Bangkok's ubiquitous rowhouses, with their layers of colourful pattern formed by signage, metal gates, doors and windows. "For me it's about looking through these layers to see something beyond, something totally different in the background." Having studied art before textiles, Lawana focuses on imagery when creating textiles. She describes fabric design as a process of 'painting in threads'.

Since her days at Mae Fah Luang, Lawana has worked on interior design and custom textiles for the Lawana Resort and Villa Lawana, Samui Island properties her father built and named after her. She has also designed products for the gift shop at Maruekhathayawan Palace, the incomparable seaside residence built by King Rama VI during the 1920s in Cha-Am. In the future she plans to create textiles from the inside out, starting with design of new yarns and threads, mixing high-tech materials with natural fibres.

"A good designer is someone who can reflect all her thoughts in design."

THIS PAGE AND OPPOSITE: **ESSENCE OF THE EARTH COLLECTION, 2004.** *Cotton.* These designs were inspired by the botanical colours and textures of dry grass, leaves and seeds found during Thailand's hot season.

"WHEN MY PROFESSOR TURNED 60 SHE SAID
SHE HAD TO SEE DOUBLE-IKAT MADE IN THAILAND BEFORE
SHE DIES, OR SHE COULD NOT CLOSE HER EYES.
THIS WAS MY GIFT TO HER."

SASIWAN DUMRONGSIRI
of Chabatik

WARP AND WEFT One of Bangkok's finest examples of a neo-traditional design approach is the silk that Sasiwan Dumrongsiri creates for her studio Chabatik. These hand-loomed textiles express both modern and antique features in nearly equal balance. The bold, semi-abstract patterns are the contemporary side of the design. The traditional part is not merely handweaving—all Thai silk has to be manually woven, due to the local yarn's irregular texture—but rather the ancient fabric-dying technique known as ikat, instantly recognisable by the handsome jagged edges it produces in the pattern.

Ikat is made by resist-dying the threads in patterns before they are woven on the loom. The threads are arranged in long bundles, laid out flat as they will stand in the finished cloth. Patterns are produced by tying the bundles with impermeable threads or strips of banana leaf or rubber, then dipping them in dye, a process that can be repeated many times with different colours to create complex designs. The dyed threads then need to be positioned precisely on the loom to render the pattern. This technique has long been practised in many places around the world. Besides South America and Africa, it was done in ancient India, from where it probably spread to Central Asia, Persia, Cambodia, Thailand, Japan and the Indonesian archipelago (which provided the Malay word *ikat*, meaning to bind, the term now used around the world to describe this cloth).

Ikat is usually done by patterning only the weft threads, or sometimes the warp, but rarely both. Double-ikat textiles like Sasiwan's, in which both the warp and weft are tie-dyed, are especially beautiful, with vivid, multi-dimensional designs. But they are so painstaking to produce that they have

OPPOSITE: **DANCING PEACOCK, 2004.** *Ikat-dyed silk.* Inspired by the sight of a peacock standing in sunlight, this pattern won the grand prize in Silpakorn University's Designer of the Year competition in 2004.

traditionally been costly luxuries associated with royalty, even with magical properties. Among the world's very few examples of double-ikat fabrics are certain *kusari* cloths of Japan, the *geringsing* crafted in one tiny village in Bali, and the fabled *patan patola* cloth of Gujarat, India, one of the most expensive textiles in the world. Their rarity owes to the dexterity, ingenuity and precision required in each stage of their production, from tying the thread bundles and dying them, to fixing them on the loom and finally the weaving itself. Even slight deviation will ruin the design.

Double-ikat had never been done in Thailand until Sasiwan came along. While studying classical Thai architecture as an undergraduate at Silpakorn University, she became interested in the costume depicted in 19th-century temple murals, which later inspired her to write a pioneering master's degree thesis on the patterns of traditional northern Thai textiles. In 1988, she founded her firm, Chabatik, intending to benefit villagers by making their hand-loomed fabrics more marketable using her original designs, first in hand-printed batik fabrics, then weft ikat silk, known as *mud-mee* in Thai. In 1992, she took up a challenge from her longtime mentor,

textile professor Nisa Sheanakul, to try to produce double-ikat, or *mud-mee son*. After two years of difficult work in collaboration with her silk weavers in Isan, Sasiwan finally succeeded.

Sasiwan sketches her designs by hand, often during the travels that inspire her poetic imagery. Later she renders the sketch on computer and prints out the design on paper for her craftspeople to dye into silk threads. Her colours are bold in a modern way, but they also recall some of the uncanny combinations seen in traditional arts such as Siamese temple ornament, especially mural painting and glass mosaic. She often uses figures from nature—birds, flowers, the sun and moon—but her imagery is done larger, bolder and less geometrically than in traditional ikat textiles.

FROM LEFT TO RIGHT: **SUN & MOON, 2004; YO-YO, 2004; SHADOWS ON WATER, 2004; LIGHT OF THE HALF MOON, 2004.** *Ikat-dyed silk. 55 x 200 cm.* Sasiwan hand-sketches designs before graphing them on computer. She issues each pattern in a limited edition, sometimes later releasing new colour combinations.

OPPOSITE: **CRESCENT AND CIRCLE, 2004.** *Ikat-dyed silk.*

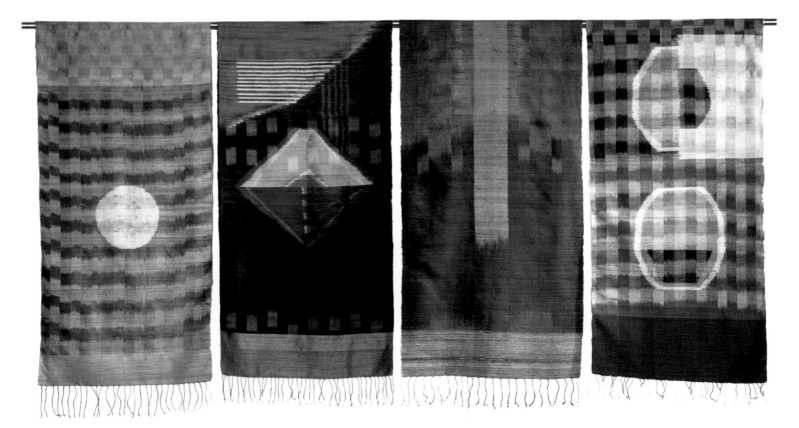

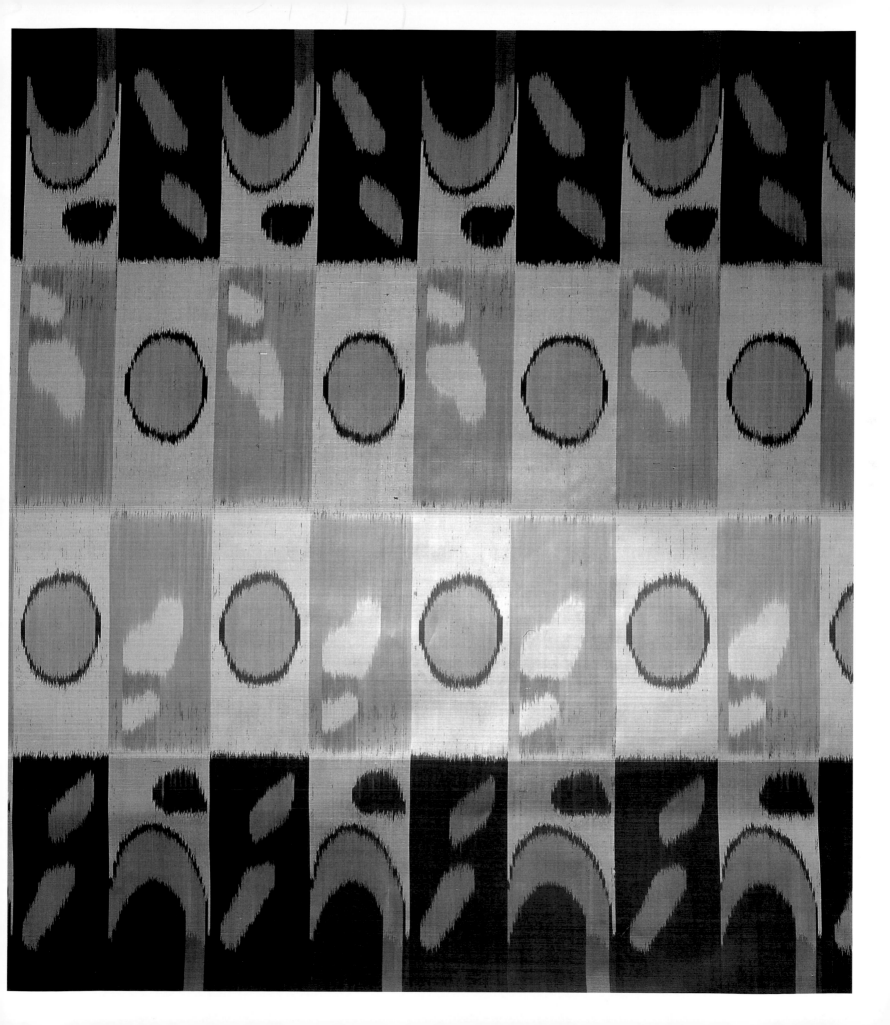

JRUMCHAI SINGALAVANIJ & WORRACHAI SIRIWIPANAN
of Pasaya

TECH EDGE Pasaya is proving that Thai designers are as savvy with technology and synthetic materials as they are with craft and naturals. The company making the brand, Satin Textile Co., has invested heavily in the most up-to-date Jacquard looms and other sophisticated equipment for spinning, dying, weaving and finishing textiles. These machines are the artistic tools for Jrumchai Singalavanij, Worrachai Siriwipanan and their 12 team members who create the kinds of extremely complex, multi-layered, three-dimensional fabrics that hand weavers could never approximate.

Jrumchai, who joined the firm in 1996 after studying textile design at Chulalongkorn University, is a gifted colourist, with the Bangkok flair for making improbable combinations succeed. "I love to see him work because at first his experiments look odd, but it all comes out beautifully in the end," Worrachai says. "He might use pastels, with vivid colours and taupe, brown and green all at the same time. It looks surprising but everything is there for a reason."

OPPOSITE: **MOVE, 2002.** *Cotton, nylon, polyester.* Jrumchai's multi-layered design won the top prize in Belgium's Decosit textile exhibition in 2002.

ABOVE: Jrumchai (left) and Worrachai head a team of 12 that creates some 500 designs a year. (Photo by Brian Mertens)

Despite his team's prolific output—at least 500 designs a year, in as many as 36 colours each—Jrumchai sometimes devotes up to eight weeks working on just a single yarn to get the effect he wants. In one experiment to develop a new palette, he sent assistants around town with colour cards to document the exact hues of certain Bangkok temples. "Using our culture is an easy way to innovate because we have it in hand. But we have to handle it carefully, to give it Pasaya's own view, something different from others. We might turn it into something very funky, very hard rock," Jrumchai says. This kind of thinking has twice won him the top prize at Belgium's Decosit textile design exhibition, the world's leading event of its kind.

Worrachai, who joined in 2004, has a more understated approach to colour, influenced by his years spent in England, where he took a master's degree in textile design at Birmingham Institute of Art and Design. "His style is quite contemporary but delicate, rich in detail and fresh," Jrumchai says. Among Worrachai's recent local sources of inspiration have been the textures of uncommon tropical fruits, the elaborate costumes of traditional Siamese *khon* court dancers, and Chinese paintings, which he uses in abstract, not traditional, ways. As he sees it, "When you are trying to come up with a style that suits the current mood of the market, it's like writing a play. Each design is like a character, and there are both stars and supporting roles. I do some with lots of emotion, some to make people smile. We have to put in lots of humour."

Managing director Schle Woodthanan used to design more fabrics himself, but now relies mostly on Jrumchai and Worrachai. "Of the many leading textile designers I've met in Europe, these two are second to none," he says. The firm was established in 1986 by Schle's father, an immigrant from a Teochew district in southern China, who named it *Saeng Chai*, or Light of Victory. Armed with two degrees in textiles from the United States, Schle built the firm up from contract manufacturing into its current strengths in technology and design, with some 1,200 employees and a suburban campus with award-winning architecture by an Italian firm. He launched Pasaya as the firm's own brand, with its own retail galleries. Some 97 per cent of production is interior textiles, 70 per cent of it exported to Europe, the United States, Australia and other overseas markets.

OPPOSITE, CLOCKWISE FROM TOP LEFT:
MARAYA, 2002. *Cotton, polyester.* Many Pasaya fabrics celebrate retro styles, like this reversible pattern with a neo-1960s look designed by Jrumchai.

TOFFEE, 2004. *Polyester.* Jrumchai's 'found' design quotes the form of a wrapped piece of toffee candy. He created this multilayered drapery fabric to take advantage of new production technology.

DHYANA, 2006. *Silk, cotton.* Pasaya designs, such as this pattern by Worrachai, sometimes cite Chinese influences.

MARAYA, 2002. *Cotton, polyester.* Jrumchai's retro design has roots in the 1950s.

"Among peoples in Asia, Thais are a bit like Italians—we are known for being lovers of beauty. I think this love of beauty will help us succeed," says Schle.

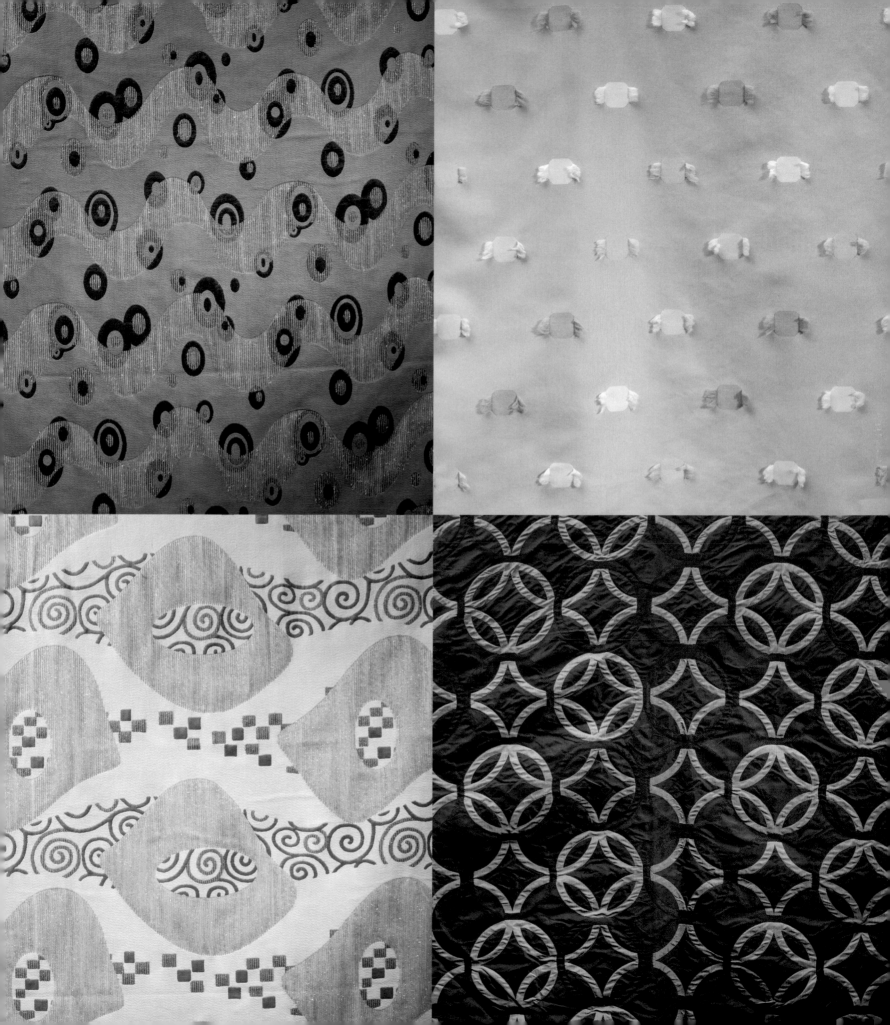

MONTRI TOEMSOMBAT

ABOVE: **COCOON: THE RENAISSANCE, 1999.** *Installation detail: silkworms, raw silk, cocoons, mannequin.* Montri's two-year project allowed silk caterpillars to create spun fabric themselves rather than unreeling cocoons and weaving the fibre by hand or by machine, a symbolic comment on sustainability. (Photo courtesy of the artist)

OPPOSITE: **FAKE ME, 2002.** *Performance: barbed wire, corrugated zinc, live dove.* Portraying himself as a human 'bonsai' tree, the artist stood cocooned in barbed wire in a performance/installation critiquing the artificiality of life in Japan, and increasingly in Bangkok.

TRANSCENDENTAL Artists can lead designers in vital new directions, usually by developing materials, forms and styles adaptable to the decorative arts. The best artists do more, however, by encouraging designers, and the rest of us as well, to see the world with enhanced vision, an intangible product that can endure longer than a material one.

A prime example is Montri Toemsombat, a rice farmer's son who has become an urbane poet of installation, video, performance art and conceptual design. With a distinctly Buddhist conscience, Montri speaks on matters of universal significance: the loss of rural culture, the folly of consumerism, the privations of urban life, the potential for artistic and human renewal. One strand woven throughout his oeuvre is the use of textiles, almost always of an experimental nature, designed not to serve practical needs but to raise questions.

Growing up in his village in Chaiyaphum province, in Thailand's economically poor but culturally rich north-east, Montri enjoyed helping his grandmother raise silkworms, often taking some to hatch into moths. This presaged his 1998–1999 project *Cocoon: The Renaissance*, in which he created alternative textiles and garments by allowing silkworms to spin fabric themselves, then letting them hatch and fly away. This poetic outcome contrasts with conventional sericulture, in which the cocoons are boiled in water to kill the larva before unwinding the strands to be spun into yarn. Montri displayed his silk in an exhibition and 'fashion' show, meant as a commentary on making consumerism less destructive of the natural world.

Silk farming has taken heat from animal rights activists, but Montri did not intend *Cocoon* as a protest. He reveres the tradition of sericulture and accepts that the creatures must be sacrificed in the process. Rather, his two-year-long experiment was a symbolic statement on how creativity can overcome ecological constraints. *Cocoon* made available a message that might be read by a sensitive designer or manufacturer as an inspiration to work toward greener practices. We as consumers might be induced to seek out furnishings made from renewable materials, as more and more Thai products are. Montri himself adapted his process to produce rough silk for actual runway fashions. By strutting his work on the catwalk, he tried to bring the persuasive power of art to audiences who don't necessarily visit galleries. This won him the Thai government's Designer of the Year award in 1999, a remarkable feat for someone never schooled in design, who had never before practised it.

In an earlier experiment with textiles, *Rice/Life* (1997–1999), Montri fashioned cloth and garments from rice seedlings. Studying art at Bangkok's elite Chulalongkorn University on scholarship during the height of Thailand's bubble years in the early 1990s, the farmer's son noticed young Thais' addiction to fashion, their effort to forge identity through clothes. So he created conceptual garments expressing his own rural identity. In a metaphor reminiscent of Buddhist parables about desire and material attachment, Montri's project compared the life of the human being to a seedling of rice. His textiles displayed rice sprouts entangled in a fabric mesh, just as Bangkok's fashion slaves had enmeshed themselves in consumerism. As ever in Montri's work, textile, text and message were interwoven. The cocoon form

and experimental textiles showed up again in a magisterial 2002 installation and performance, *Fake Me*, the outcome of a half-year residency in Fukuoka, Japan, which presented Montri's dreamlike vision of three Japanese traditional art forms: the bonsai tree, the zen stone garden and haiku poetry. Montri covered a Bangkok gallery floor with corrugated zinc, a harsh, industrial facsimile of the pattern of raked stones seen in zen gardens like Kyoto's Ryoanji. He installed a bonsai tree fashioned from barbed wire (itself a form of textile), built a metal shed like a temple hall or squatter's hut, and hung silk tapestries embroidered with verses of his own poetry. For the exhibition opening, the artist cocooned himself naked in a costume made of barbed wire. For several painful hours, he stayed trapped there, clutching a live white dove in his motionless hands, prevented from speaking by a barbed-wire gag in his mouth. This eloquent effort he dubbed his 'Portrait of the Artist as a Young Bonsai.'

Fake Me was a both poignant and ironic comment on cultural malaise—the relentless artificiality of Japan's urban environment, its regimented social order. Montri compared the individual in Japanese society to a bonsai tree, something natural that is restrained by the artifice of training wires and pruning. His use of metal jabbed at the coldness of Japanese cities. Aiming beyond Japan's dystopia, *Fake Me* pointed at countries like Thailand speeding down the same path of reckless modernisation.

Since that show, Montri's work has continued to explore questions of cultural and artistic identity, through works involving nature, textiles and texts, as well as new areas like meditation, often with audience participation.

OPPOSITE: **RICE/LIFE, 1997–1999.** *Dried rice seedlings on fabric.* Montri questioned Bangkok's fashion obsession using an 'alternative textile' rooted in his childhood on a rice farm. (Photo courtesy of the artist)

FOLLOWING PAGE: **FAKE ME, 2002.** *Installation detail: wire mesh, corrugated zinc.* The installation offered a haunting vision of alienation.

PAGE 155 : **COCOON: THE RENAISSANCE, 1999.** *Spun silk fabric.* (Photo courtesy of the artist)

"THE CONCEPTS OF MY PROJECTS ARE DRAWN FROM THE CULTURE OF ISAN, THE NORTHEASTERN PART OF THAILAND WHERE I GREW UP. THROUGH MY ART, I TRY TO DEVELOP THE ESSENCE OF MY RURAL ROOTS IN ORDER TO LINK IT TO THE CONTEMPORARY PERIOD AND TO OPEN THE SEEDS OF THIS HERITAGE INTO THE ARTISTIC PANORAMA OF THE FUTURE."

CUSTOM DESIGN ∎ **Reflections Rooms** ∎ **Prima Chakrabandhu na Ayudhya**

"Deco, style and spirit reflect the taste of the fantasyful creative temper of each designer and will definitive satisfy art lovers... A place away from the contemporary global style—a place for fantasy and made your dreams come true."

REFLECTIONS ROOMS
by Anusorn Ngernyuang & friends

INN VERSION As growing numbers of 'hip' hotels cater to what they call 'highly individual people', the hotels themselves begin to look curiously alike. Even the so-called art hotel is, from a free-thinking Thai point of view, another boutique hotel dressed up in paintings. Leave it to an intrepid innkeeper like Anusorn Ngernyuang, son of a horror novelist and Bangkok's foremost purveyor of kitsch accessories (page 112), to take an indelicate step beyond these concepts.

One day in 2003, Anusorn found a 1960s apartment block in a shabby-genteel neighbourhood, and knew right away it was time to put his life savings in jeopardy. Nudging 28 artistically inclined friends—fashion designers, art directors, painters and film producers—he asked each to do up a room. Anusorn would pay them not with money but with creative freedom—the chance to let their imaginations run wild. Thus began Anusorn's own horror story. The artistes took months just getting started, then ran wild with the budget. But the story came to a happy ending: an artists' hotel that reflects Bangkok's own individuality and space.

Perhaps too spicy for some corporate clients, Anusorn confides. "The modeling agencies beg me, 'Please, put my models in your plain rooms. They have to shoot in the morning—I want them fresh!' Some of our suites are, you know, very pink. I always wonder if they'll be able to survive the kitsch."

So far, guests have not just survived the kitsch but lapped it up. The multiple decor concepts entice repeat visits: switching rooms makes 30 stays seem like 30 different hotels. There are a few interiors by renowned Czech designers like Borek Sipek, but more daring are the suites designed by Thais, rich in what the Reflections literature rightly calls 'the fantasyful creative temper of each designer'.

The hotel's brochure itself is fantasyful. Anusorn parodies the studied, pretentious air of design hotels by writing the copy himself and leaving his giddy English unedited, letting it help set a holiday mood. Guests choose their rooms after reading this expressive bit of Bangkok style, which is the source of the quotes in large type in this chapter.

PRINCESS KITSCH

This rather lush room was created by Anna Smith, an English designer of kitsch accessories. Smith envisioned a shrine to her idol, authoress Dame Barbara Cartland, the late Queen of Romance whose 723 books, including *Wings of Ecstasy* and *The Windmill of Love*, sold more than 1 billion copies. Famous for her love of pink, Dame Cartland once told a fan, "If you're not gaudy, no one will notice you." This room is noticeable for its generous use of magenta chinoiserie, roses, hearts and fleur-de-lys.

"The sweetest room for a joyful princess. Decorated with colourful kitsch and fun stuff. The private room that is suitable for a young lady."

POST INDUSTRIAL

Reflection's most inventive room is also its most inexpensively constructed, made from reclaimed junkyard materials and ordinary objects from the hardware store. Crafted by abstract painter Thaiwijit Poengkasemsomboon, the room embodies his sense of the offbeat beauty of the artefacts of industry. The palette is coolly subdued, centering on the neutral tones of cement, metal, unfinished wood, half-painted plasterboard and exposed brick. Accent colours glint from the ceramic tiles of the shower platform in pastels, the window curtain in gem-like hues, and an exposed water pipe in powder green.

The recycled elements are rich in textures softened and warmed by long use, the same aesthetics seen in Thaiwijit's many designs for lamps and pots (page 100). He sculpted almost all the fixtures himself, including the sink made from an old chair, Eero Saarinen's classic Tulip design. It all functions well. Light switches, tables, seats and shelves are optimally positioned. The open layout creates a luxuriously wide space from a small room, thanks to the low horizon created by sinking the bed into the floor.

BOHEMIAN RHAPSODY

"AWAY FROM THE BOURGEOIS LIFE, FEEL THE IMPRESSIONISTS SPIRIT AND GIPSY MOOD."

Marcel Georg Mueller is one of those global nomads ever in search of the world's liveliest night life and trendiest trends. Swiss, but not *too* Swiss, Mueller conceived his room as a gypsy's tent pitched in Bangkok, drenched in colour and kitsch.

PRETTY IN PINK

The guest room designed by Anusorn himself is a kind of sleep-in art gallery, shown here paneled in hand-painted copies of portraits by Colombian artist Fernando Botero, each available for purchase: buxom Mona Lisas, plump matadors and hirsute transvestites.

"In the name of Rose: Simple by the idea, but completely outraged of the everyday boring blue. With hundreds of various paintings that can be changed for every mood."

THE ART OF LOVE

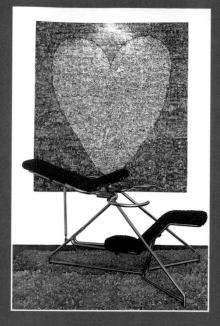

Artist Chalit Nakpawan takes a cheeky look at the tradition of the love hotel, creating an interior that mates romance with mischief. He highlights a palette of gem colours by using white brick walls and glossy black wooden floors. His open floorplan creates lots of space, with a free-standing shower in the middle of the room. "I was thinking of a gallery, everything clean and white, with splashes of paint. In an open space, everything is relaxed.... With the shower in the middle, it's very sexy—you can watch your girlfriend. Maybe you can have sex together in the shower, and the coloured light shines in through the glass to make you happy," says Chalit, son of a fruit farmer from Samut Songkhram province, and well known for his paintings, ceramics and sculpture.

Guests can enhance the pleasures of their stay by utilising Chalit's twist on a piece of steel furniture manufactured in Thailand specially for the ergonomics of love hotels. The artist added upholstery in fake red fur to brighten the mood, and hung his painting of a heart nearby. "When I think about sex, everything is so good, so relaxed, so cute—and a little bit naughty."

"EROTIC AMAZING: WHAT IS LOVE? WHAT DO YOU EXPECT FROM LOVE? SEX, ROMANCE, DESIRE, FANTASY OR WHAT'S ELSE? YOU CAN FIND IT IN THIS ROOM."

POP INN

"THE VERY CLEAN & CLEAR ROOM BY WHITE COLOURED WALLS WILL MAKE THE VISITOR FEEL DEEPLY PEACEFUL. AND BREATH THE EXCITEMENT OF REAL POP-ART FROM THE ORIGINAL ARTIST MR. KONGPAT."

This bright and airy room was created by Kongpat Sakdapitak, a sunny personality celebrated for his frisky paintings and pop handicrafts. Son of a rice farmer from the north-eastern province of Loei, Kongpat won a national art competition at the age of eight and has been painting ever since. For Reflections, he conceived a room as a kind of walk-in frame for a three-dimensional painting. Arriving at the project site with no plan in mind, he executed the work in just three hours, choosing a colour scheme based on scraps of paper left on the floor by construction workers. The main room features a row of colourful cocktails standing on a trompe l'oeil wrap-around bar.

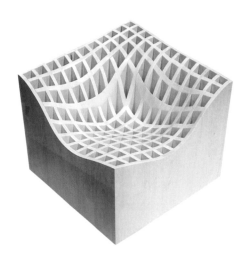

THIS PAGE: Eggarat Wongcharit's wooden Vasarely chair, 2006, for Crafactor, combines flowing lines and a grid-like structure, while Crafactor's Sarong chaise lounge by Paiwate Wangbon expresses flowing lines in dyed water hyacinth braid on a fibreglass base (photos courtesy of Crafactor).

OPPOSITE: Temples are guarded by the *naga* figures carved on roof eaves. Sukhothai-era Buddha images express grace through languid lines; a seated figure touches the ground to invoke the Buddha's moment of enlightenment, while walking figures of Buddhist disciples express a meditative posture in motion.

Flowing Lines
The preferred path between two Thai points is often a curve.

The sinuosity of many Bangkok designs recalls the lines of traditional Thai art, which tend not to march but flow. The exemplary feature of northern Thai religious architecture, for example, is a long balustraded stairway approaching a temple gate or door, undulating like the primordial form it embodies, the *naga* water serpent, a mythical guardian creature with benign powers. Architect and writer Dr Sumet Jumsai traces *nagas* to the water-borne origins of South-east Asian civilisation, which flourished near waterways for transport, fishing and irrigation (as it still does). The *naga* figures that have long decorated things like temple roofs and royal barge prows nowadays rear their heads on things like truck ornaments and the necks of electric guitars.

Sinuous form ripples through other art as well. The central Siamese culture of the ancient kingdom of Sukhothai is epitomised by its 'walking' Buddha images, graceful figures sculpted in the 14th and 15th centuries. They seem to float, transcending corporeality and gender. In the 17th and 18th centuries, the rectangular layout of Buddhist chapels was softened by the bowed, shiplike shape of their bases, another marine reference. Thai decorative motifs,

lai thai, are assembled from curving lines. These are the designs inscribed in carved wood, plasterwork, lacquer painting and other arts that define Siamese classical style.

Folk culture features curves in things like the concave roofs and tapering finials of Siamese houses. Dome-like roofs cover wagons and howdahs, the seats used on elephants. In everyday popular culture, the lines can be traced in the elaborate coiffures of society women, and the metal decorations on trucks and *tuk-tuks*, Thailand's signature three-wheeled taxis.

What is distinctive about these Thai lines is their rationale, which is aesthetic, not structural. They do not embody nature in an organic or realistic way, but abstract it, stylise it, embellish it, elongate it, give it flair. They don't stand against nature, but just beyond it (often depicting celestials).

Makers of furnishings might take these cosmic references as a style caveat; it can be risky to extend traditional lines into modern design. Restraint is usually needed, so that Thai lines can express flair and feeling, rather than elaborateness. This appropriateness has been mastered by Suwan Kongkhunthian, designer of Yothaka furniture.

OPPOSITE: **Siamese 'living room'. An absence of furniture is one of the comforts of the traditional Thai house on stilts. The central terrace is a multi-purpose outdoor 'room' used for meals, chores, ceremonies, recreation and rest. The triangular 'axe' cushion seen in the background is used to recline (photo by Photobank).**

THIS PAGE: **At top, Eggarat Wongcharit's rattan All of Me ottoman/coffee table, 2000, can be inverted and filled with its four floor cushions to serve as a seat (photo courtesy of Crafactor). At left, Jitrin Jintaprecha's Tung Seatable, 2003 serves as side table, ottoman or a low table used while sitting on the floor (photo courtesy of Stone & Steel). At right, Jitrin demonstrates his round Klom Coffee Seatable, a multi-use solution with built-in shelf for floor cushions (photo courtesy of Stone & Steel).**

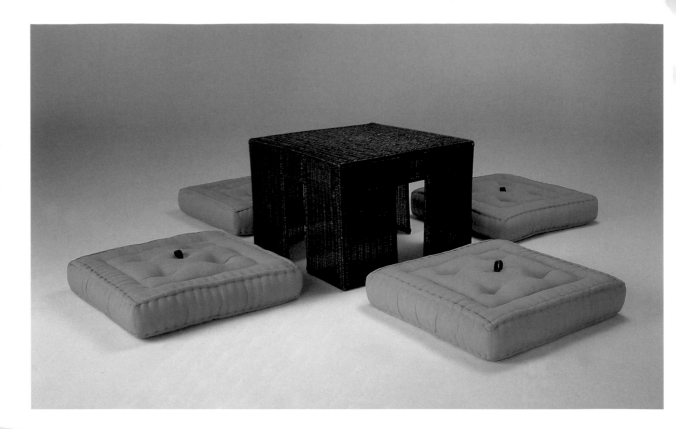

Floor Seating

An unfussy custom grounded in practicality and the body.

One powerful local design influence is the traditional practice of sitting on the floor. While Westerners have long perched on seats built a standard 43 centimetres above the ground, furniture was little used in Thailand until the 1950s, and floor seating still prevails in rural homes. Temple-goers sit on the floor, at a level below the monks seated on low tables or chairs.

At home, the practical advantages of floor seating are many. A small space becomes less cluttered. Without tables and chairs to define how a room should be used, it can take on multiple functions more flexibly, as a place to work, care for children, eat meals, socialise, sleep. Floor cushions and mats cost less than wooden or upholstered furniture.

A related idea is the practice of sitting on low platforms. The low table around which people sit on the floor—usually a Chinese-influenced *tang*, with curved legs—can instead serve as a surface on which to sit, recline or sleep. Outdoors, platforms made of split bamboo or timber are used for resting above the damp and insects on the ground. These de facto daybeds are usually positioned under the shade of trees or eaves made of palm thatch. They serve as standard equipment in the breezy, multi-purpose open space

under the floor of the traditional Siamese house on stilts.

Beyond practicality, there are social and health advantages to floor and platform seating. It is informal, intimate and communal. Inherently family-friendly, it allows a small group to become a large group and then small again, as members come and go while meals are eaten, games are played, children are tended. The floor forms a clean surface for sitting because one removes shoes before entering the house. In the view of some ergonomics experts like Galen Cranz, author of *The Chair: Rethinking Culture, Body and Design*, floor seating allows better alignment of the spine than Western-style furniture. Sitting on the floor, you can adjust your posture freely and position cushions for support.

All of this suits stressed-out urbanites who want domestic furnishings that promote relaxation and a sense of being in touch with one's body and companions. Thai designers are offering low-slung chairs, big cushions and other furnishings conducive to floor seating. The approach can be practical, like a floor-hugging table that doubles as a seat to make flexible use of a small space. Or it can be luxurious, like daybeds and oversized chairs that encourage the sitter to draw up the feet and take ease.

Natural Materials
Mother Earth's design potential continues to grow.

Natural materials are one of Thailand's two primary design resources, alongside craft. Local designers, living in a society still rooted in agriculture, understand the materials in a way that foreigners rarely can. The handicrafts still used in everyday life demonstrate the aesthetics, performance and sustainability of the natural things from which they are made. These design merits are getting renewed attention from materials scientists like Dr Andrew Dent of global consultancy Material ConneXion, who says "Nature has an ability to create things out of nothing that have a resilience, durability and aesthetic appeal beyond anything we can dream of."

Thailand's rich soil, ample rain and strong sun support far more species of cultivated and wild plants than grow in temperate climates, and at faster rates of growth. There are some 1,500 species of trees, as well as grasses like bamboo and vetiver, and vines like *lipao* and rattan. These materials become myriad handcrafted tools, textiles and buildings. In craft and design alike, natural materials serve in weaving, cushioning, structuring, ornamenting and colouring.

Applied in design, naturals can offer sustainable characteristics like renewability, biodegradability and non-toxicity. They add aesthetic qualities like texture, colour, fragrance and warmth. At their best, they have a power to evoke memories and emotions associated with place.

The design potential for natural materials is still being expanded. Scientist Dent states that among all major categories of materials—metals, ceramics, plastics, composites, nano-technological, etc.—the one with highest potential for future development is naturals. This is one reason why Material ConneXion chose Bangkok as the location of its first Asian branch, at the Thailand Creative and Design Center, to add industrially enhanced natural materials from Thailand to its selective database.

Thailand's research and development spending is lower than in high-income countries, but a significant share is devoted to agricultural research. Universities, corporations, royal projects and non-government groups are active in scientific and technological work to advance Thailand's plant and animal resources, with special strengths in applications like tissue culturing.

In the realm of design, Bangkok's most inventive user of natural materials is Angus Hutcheson, who has innovated super-organic lamps from such unlikely materials as silk cocoons, shredded bark and palm leaves. His lamps moulded from latex take advantage of Thailand's position as the world's largest grower of rubber.

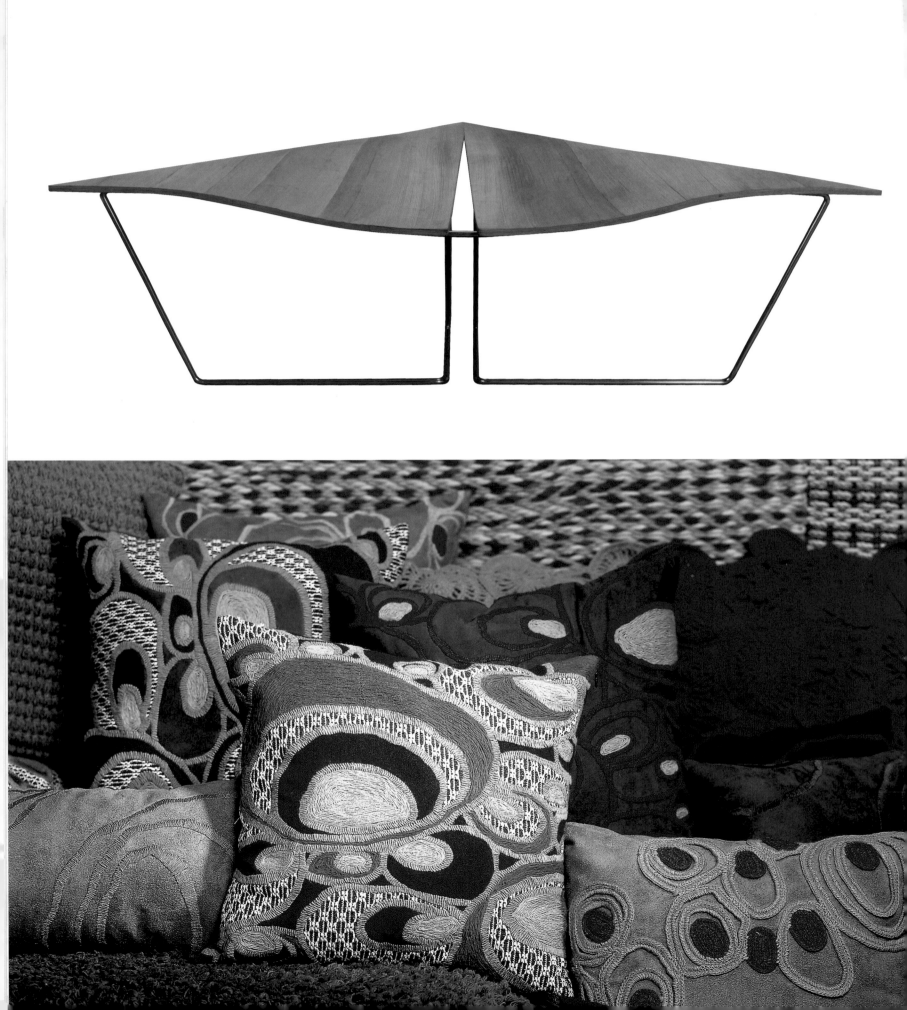

OPPOSITE: The wing-like form of the manta ray inspired Yommana Taninpong's Kra-Bain seat for Stone & Steel, created in a 2006 Department of Export Promotion workshop (photo courtesy of DEP). Ploenchan Vinyaratn explores the patterns and colours of a coral reef in her Beneath the Blue textile collection for Beyond Living.

THIS PAGE: Thailand's favourite animal inspired Bangkok's Elephant Tower. Singh Intrachooto's Chairwalker seat for Osisu is made of scraps of wood reclaimed from manufacturing processes (photo courtesy of Osisu).

Animal Motifs
The design logic of the zoological.

Species diversity, sometimes cited as a resource for industries like eco-tourism and pharmaceuticals research, is rarely mentioned as an asset for design. But in Thailand both age-old crafts and contemporary designs show how animals can—in their shapes, markings, even behaviour—suggest ideas for decorative arts, often with readymade good proportions and lines. Animal motifs also serve auspicious purposes, like the 12 creatures that herald the 12 years of the Asian zodiac.

Thailand is crawling with some 1,700 known species of amphibians, birds, mammals and reptiles, compared to just 750 in a temperate country of similar size like France, according to the World Conservation Monitoring Centre. Compared to France, people here live in closer proximity to animals, even in the city, with its mahout-driven elephants, back-alley chicken coops and innumerable street dogs.

This abundance is mirrored in crafts, where animals appear in traditional textile patterns, and the shapes of objects like decorative boxes. Coconut graters are carved into animal shapes—rabbits, dogs, mice—a bit of *sanook* to lighten the chore of scraping meat from the fruit. Temples are decorated in animal designs, rich in symbolism, sometimes exuberantly stylised.

In contemporary design, curved animal forms can be adapted to create seating with good ergonomics. An animal's geometry is readily understandable, and easily scaled to human proportions. Zoological shapes are unusual but not alienating. As Thai designers seem to intuit, animal designs have an inherent market appeal. This fact is suggested by studies of wine sales in the United States, where bottles featuring animal motifs sell twice as well as others, according to AC Nielsen research. The approach can quote the animal in total, like Preeda Siripornsub's Dolphin chair (page 72), or abstract a bit of pattern or shape, like Ploenchan Vinyaratn's textiles in butterfly and coral reef designs.

LOCAL INITIATIVES

The Mosaic Method

Improvisation Empowers A New Thai Industry

Design offers unexpected but authentic insights into Thai culture. It's more than how the designs themselves—their materials, craftsmanship and inspiration—convey a spirit of place. More telling of Thailand today is how these furnishings have come about. Designers have turned their ideas into products, companies and the beginnings of a design movement in ways that reveal how Thais tend to do things—especially the Thai way of beating the odds.

And the odds are still against design here. Manufacturers are typically weak on product innovation. Foreign-owned factories make foreign-designed products for foreign brands. Local plants have lower levels of technology. They tend to imitate foreign products, or view design as mere styling, a gimmick to boost sales. Many Thai firms just produce on contract using international customers' own design blueprints. Designers who want to use sophisticated materials and components often have to import them, an obstacle in developing prototypes. Design education is weak, and the local market for design products is small. Piracy is huge.

Yet, thanks to local ingenuity—a Thai gift for improvisation and adaptation—designers have managed to express themselves in ways that are winning acclaim and commercial success. This resourcefulness is the real Thainess of Thai design today. And it is never more Thai than when designers turn a liability into an asset, a constraint into an opportunity.

One example is the way so many designers transform their lack of industrial design education into an advantage. Before delving into furnishings to survive the economic crisis after 1997, most of them were working in fields like architecture, art, advertising and engineering. So they took skills and concepts from their old professions and adapted them to making products. As a result, Bangkok designers don't necessarily follow the latest agenda taught at Western design schools, but what they might lack in methodical and conceptual rigour, they gain in seeing with fresh eyes, in sketching with a free hand. They work more from intuition than system. The things around them—Thai things especially—become their inspiration. It's about provisional methods, piecing together ready solutions.

OPPOSITE: **WAT ARUN.** 19th-century artisans turned broken ceramics into a Buddhist memorial that also stands as a monument of Thai innovation.

"This is the Thai way of thinking. We always try to find a way around the problem," says architect Duangrit Bunnag. Likewise furniture designer Eggarat Wongcharit writes of Thai designers' talent for finding 'hidden treasure'—surviving a design environment of seeming deprivation by uncovering the resources buried right under their feet.

Designers find ways around the manufacturing problem, for example. The obstacle is that most local factories are either too large, too inflexible or too technologically backward to make quality design products on contract. So designers start their own factories. They do this as much by necessity as by choice, but it offers inherent advantages. With limited capital, their companies start small and rarely grow larger than 100 employees, so they focus on production quality rather than quantity, targeting high-end niches. Designers gain authorship over their products; they call the shots. They can collaborate closely with craftspeople and technicians. Their firms can't afford laser-cutting devices or imported high-tech materials, but local technologies and materials often perform better, with far more charm. Bangkok design celebrates craft construction, natural materials and reclaimed elements.

This kind of resourcefulness is ad hoc but not accidental. Thai culture has its deepest roots in animism, an unsystematic belief system that is flexible and provisional. This worldview, like that of Hinduism and Buddhism which later shaped the culture, translates into an improvisational approach to problems—a talent for adaptability, cultural eclecticism and ready-made solutions.

You can see this approach in Siamese architecture. Consider Wat Arun (page 195), the Temple of Dawn, the monumental spire that symbolises Bangkok. Despite its massiveness, this tower has a feeling of lightness and life, thanks in part to its covering of colourful ceramics that catch the sun's changing rays all day. When the tower was built in the 19th-century, Siam could not produce the kinds of fine porcelain and brightly coloured glazes that kilns in China could, and so crockery was imported.

Ceramics broken during shipment did not go to waste; Bangkok craftsmen chiseled the fragments into bits of mosaic. Set into architectural stucco in floral and geometric designs, this crockery mosaic served as an improvised form of ornament superior to purpose-made decorations because the ceramic glazes could endure the tropical sun, keeping their colour. It's a local ingenuity that recalls the saying, "If life gives you lemons, make lemonade". Turn something sour into something sweet, a shattered saucer into something whole again.

Today, furnishings designers turn sour to sweet in the way they handle piracy. Thailand was long notorious for counterfeiting foreign brands, but now Thai products are being knocked-off, both at home and overseas. So Thai designers strive to innovate faster than copycats can copy, issuing new collections every six to 12 months, using materials and processes that are hard for others to adopt. In this way, they turn the problem of piracy into an impetus, letting it spur their creativity.

Designers brandish other weapons against pirates. Setting up their own factories rather than outsourcing helps them keep their trade secrets truly secret. They focus on selling into export markets where patents, trademarks and copyrights are better safeguarded. They take pirates to court to shut them down. And they stand their ground together. In 1999, ML Pawinee Santisiri founded the Design & Object Association, a group of leading firms which requires its members to practise design originality. Copycats are expelled. From just nine founding members, the association has grown to more than 90 firms.

Sufficiency economics

The Design & Object Association's members are almost all designer-entrepreneurs, and this too reflects the Thai way of doing things. It takes but a quick walk down any Bangkok street, with its flourish of sidewalk vendors and little shops, to see that entrepreneurship is deeply rooted here. Studies confirm that the desire to own a business is stronger in Thailand than in almost any country in the world. The annual Global Entrepreneurship Monitor report by London Business School and Babson College ranked Thailand among the world's top three nations in terms of entrepreneurial activity for the years 2000 through 2003. Some of that activity resulted from designers' eagerness to found their own companies.

In this way, designers helped the local economy recover from its bubble years. Thailand was walking on air from 1985 to 1995, in ways both good and bad. A decade as the world's fastest-growing economy raised the nation's income to a high, but also worsened many ills: widening gaps in income and wealth, relentless consumerism, heavy corporate reliance on debt, giddy speculation in stocks and real estate. Industry was actually declining in competitiveness; manufacturers' focus on low-cost, mass-produced goods left them vulnerable to cheaper rivals, as stagnant export figures showed. Companies were short on both innovation and quality. The baht's collapse in 1997 meant foreign money could no longer be borrowed to cover it all up.

The bubble's burst created hardship, but helped creativity. Thailand turned inward, towards native wisdom and cultural resources, while also looking outward to better cope with globalisation. Big business lost its lustre, outshone by scrappy startups eager to test new ideas. The public overcame an addiction to foreign labels and chose to buy Thai. Contemporary art came alive, now driven by concepts and social commentary rather than commerce. In pop culture, corporate product gave way to indie innovation. In politics and government, a new, reformist constitution strengthened the democratic systems instituted in 1992.

A few dozen civic leaders and public intellectuals helped promote new ideas about rejuvenating Thailand from within. Most eminent of these voices was that of Thailand's revered monarch, King Bhumibol Adulyadej. In speeches and writings—demonstrated by decades of actual practise in His Majesty's more than 3,000 rural development and environmental projects—the King counselled greater national self-reliance, and a rather Buddhist concept of a 'sufficiency economy', based in part on an ethic of moderation. Whatever the flight of foreign capital, Thailand had its own intangible capital, the economic and social resources embedded in its own way of life, history and culture. This soon became evident in design.

A big step toward product innovation had already begun in 1985 with a rural development initiative done very much in the spirit of the King's own projects—a research effort to turn an invasive floating weed called water hyacinth into design crafts that would provide an upcountry source of income for poor villagers (page 210). By 1997, the effort had spawned companies like Yothaka and Ayodhya that were weaving designer furnishings sold around the world. Other initiatives, like the Mae Fah Luang Foundation's effort to enrich hill tribe textiles with modern design, began succeeding (page 206).

Hundreds of little companies started up, and stayed up. Compared to other Thai products, the new design has better kept its head above the global flood of low-cost Chinese goods. High-end trade buyers come to exhibitions and showrooms in Bangkok, not

China, boosting sales among the quality brands by 10 to 30 per cent per year from 2000 to 2005. Thanks in part to growth by the leading Thai firms, the overall local industry has also grown. Thailand's furniture exports have risen from $755 million in 1995 to $1.2 billion in 2005, now ranking among the top 15 manufactured export product categories in value, according to Ministry of Commerce figures. Interior textiles increased from $149 million in 2001 to $240 million in 2005. Decorative accessories are too diverse to track in official figures, but the proliferation of offerings in trade shows and markets suggests they have blossomed even more.

The government has found real ways to help. In 2005, it opened a world-class resource centre, The Thailand Creative and Design Center (TCDC), to make ideas and information accessible to all Thais (page 200). The Department of Export Promotion helps with its BIG and TIFF shows, while its Product Development Center holds prototyping workshops for young designers that yield enticing results each year (including a few designs shown in this book). Other government efforts include the Fashion Trend Center and the Thailand Knowledge Park, a high-tech public library. Since 2001, the OTOP (One Tambon, One Product) campaign has helped more than 70,000 *tambon*, or villages, each identify and market its own best crafts and food products—everything from pineapple-fibre paper and bamboo furniture to specialty fruits and herbal teas. This programme follows decades of successful efforts by HM Queen Sirikit to support handicrafts throughout the country.

Designs on the future

These initiatives point toward better furnishings to come. Thai designers already excel in innovating form and using intuitive approaches to develop products. They can grow by working deeper on concept, production approaches and marketing. More will follow Eggarat Wongcharit's lead in balancing the use of craft with more use of factory processes that increase product consistency and affordability. Like him, more will branch out from natural materials into things like metal and fibreglass. As brands become more established in the international marketplace, designers may find they have less need to rely on overt Thai inspiration to get noticed abroad. The pitfall of expressing local identity in every design is the risk of making products that are more novel than innovative. Well-established designers will be empowered to explore other facets of

design that play to local strengths without trading on Thainess itself.

More designers will work on staff or on commission for big manufacturers, which are turning to design to beat Chinese competitors. Ou Baholyodhin has led the way by designing premium sanitary ware for a new Thai brand, named Nahm, launched by a contract manufacturing firm in 2002. In 2003, he created the Time series of tumblers and stemware for Ocean Glass, a big company that now offers several designer collections. Contract textile makers will follow Pasaya's lead in launching their own brands (page 148).

Thai design benefits from grass roots resources like Bangkok's tradition of open-air markets and vending in the street. Young designers and artisans can take their ideas to market literally overnight thanks to the ready availability of inexpensive retail space in prime locations like Chatuchak Market, Siam Square and the Suan Lum Night Bazaar. But many of these charming markets are threatened by gentrification. As of this writing, Suan Lum—which hosts at least 100 up-and-coming designers of furnishings, fashion and jewellery among its 3,000 shops—is slated for possible replacement by Thailand's tallest skyscraper.

Landlords are entitled to market-level rents. What is needed is a European-style public fund to preserve unique public resources like venerable markets, shophouse neighbourhoods and old buildings while compensating property owners appropriately. The cost would be less than the tens of millions of dollars the government spends on activities like advertising, special events and promotions that represent no long-term investment in the real assets that support tourism, SMEs, culture and design.

Thailand has an intriguing potential to develop its nascent strengths in sustainable design, and make this a part of its product branding. Sustainability is already built into most of the better designs, but it results more from good intentions and luck than from a systematic approach. A credible local certification system—never before attempted in Asia—would pitch Thai design to the rising sustainability requirements of contractors and retailers in Europe and the United States.

Sustainability can include social factors like treatment of workers. Much as intended by groups like Mae Fah Luang, Thai design products are helping raise the incomes of the craftspeople who make them. Some of the firms pay above-market wages, either by enlightened choice, or by sheer necessity due to Thailand's shortage of workers. Firms manufacturing outside Bangkok provide a benefit just as important as good pay: a job upcountry that lets artisans live in their own villages with their families rather than migrating to the city in search of a job. Some mothers do piece-work at home—braiding water hyacinth for furniture, raising silkworms or weaving—which lets them tend their children. A home-grown version of fair trade practices promoted by Western non-government organisations could become an explicit part of the Thai way of doing design, an element in branding, if organised and legitimised through accreditation.

Thailand has long-term potential to strengthen its design prowess as did the Nordic countries, which first earned a reputation for excellence in design crafts like furniture and ceramics before excelling in industrial design. Finland, for example, progressed from Arts and Crafts furnishings in the late 19th and early 20th centuries to modern design manufactures like Marimekko textiles and houseware in the 1950s and 1960s, to today's high-tech products like Nokia cellphones. Thais seem destined to originate more designs for the appliances, electronics, sporting goods and transport equipment already manufactured here by foreign companies.

While the Finns took a century to broaden and deepen their application of design, Bangkok is advancing with post-modern speed. Hundreds of Thais graduate from design degree programmes at home and abroad each year. Foreign manufacturers like Honda are setting up research and development centres here. Local firms are climbing up the innovation ladder. It took only three years for furniture designer Pisit Kunanantakul to adapt skills from creating minimalist seating for his brand Isolar to designing electric vehicles for manufacture by his family's large company. As Pisit testifies, "When you design furniture, you are making just one thing. But creating a car is designing 1,000 things that all have to fit together. I never thought I could do this before."

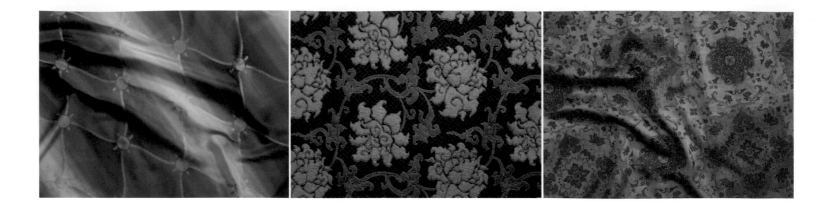

A Legend Grows
Jim Thompson and Today's Thai Silk Co.

The mystery of Jim Thompson's disappearance in 1967 remains unsolved. But one thing is clear: the American is still doing what he always did best—selling silk. In the old days, he plied it to rich travellers in the lobby of The Oriental Hotel, or to costume designers in Hollywood and Broadway. Now it's his legend that sells, helping The Thai Silk Co. grow far beyond Thompson's idealistic dreams to become one of the world's premier examples of a design crafts enterprise, with some 3,000 employees in five countries. What started in 1947 as an expatriate's experiment in organising a Bangkok cottage industry is today Thailand's best-known design brand and the world's largest maker of hand-woven fabric, including one extraordinary hand-printed textile that ranks as the world's costliest.

And yet despite the fame of its brand, the company itself remains something of a mystery. It is privately held and advertises sparingly, often simply using an old black-and-white photo of Thompson's patrician face. But beyond this smiling image, who owns and runs The Thai Silk Co. today? How did it survive after Thompson vanished while vacationing in Malaysia? How has it changed since the days when he used to set out each morning from his timber Siamese villa, rowing his skiff across a Bangkok canal to visit the neighbourhood weavers? How has hand-weaving held on in an age of globalised mega production?

Thompson's Thai story began a few days after the close of World War II, when he arrived in Bangkok as part of an advance team of the OSS, progenitor of the CIA. After his discharge, he looked for a project to stay on in Thailand. Thompson came from a privileged background, had trained and practiced as an architect in New York, and had an eye for art and antiques. He quickly noticed the outstanding qualities of Thai silk—its handsome texture and patterns. Its greatest asset was its vibrant colour, in those days especially, before the spread of synthetic yarns. But local hand weaving was being crushed by machine-made textiles from Europe, the United States and Japan.

So Thompson took up revival of this craft as an interesting social cause, hoping to profit both himself and neighbourhood weavers. He organised them into a network, upgraded their manual looms with foot-pedaled machines and replaced their traditional natural dyes with colourfast chemical dyes.

He formed his company in 1948, selling most of the shares to

RIGHT: Created in 1923, the Tree of Life design is based on an Indian motif rooted in ancient Persian precedents. Some 315 wood blocks are used to form one repeat of the pattern. Costing $1,000 or more a metre, it is the kind of fabric that decorates stately homes and palaces.

OPPOSITE: In patterns like the Jacquard-woven silk Xanadu, 2003 (left) and silk/linen Apsara, 2005 (centre), designer Tinnart Nisalak carries on his predecessor's flair for blending Oriental and Western designs. The printed silk at right is Jim Thompson's own design based on the decoration of 19th-century Siamese *benjarong* ceramics.

Thai investors, and soon began travelling the world to promote the product. At home in Bangkok too, he was an ambassador for silk. He had the independent financial means to live as a bon vivant, and his home became a magnet for socialites, diplomats, visiting writers and celebrities. The house was an attraction in itself. In 1959 he bought half a dozen antique wooden Siamese homes, and set them up in a palatial, gardened compound, filling the interiors with Asian antiques.

He was a good American salesman, well-connected, and skilled in the art of product placement. He introduced Thai silk to the likes of *Vogue* editor Edna Woolman Chase, and put it on stage in costumes for the Broadway musical, *The King and I*. It decorated posh interiors like Windsor Castle.

Roman gladiators played a role, as well. In 1958, Thompson visited the set of the movie *Ben Hur*. The actors griped that their costumes looked too refined for military garb, so Thompson delivered a bulky silk to better match imperial armour. The film won 11 Oscars, including one for best colour costume design, and rescued MGM Studio from bankruptcy. The fabric itself became a hit. Made from a sturdy six-ply thread, its heavier bulk helped silk play a new role in upholstery and curtains, and it is still the brand's leading weight.

The problem Thai silk had in 1947—being handmade—is today its asset. Thai silk is different from varieties cultivated elsewhere—the fibre is naturally uneven, so it cannot be woven by machine. The weaver's care is needed to keep the thread from breaking. Even the fastest craftswoman can loom only five or six yards of the fabric each day, and complicated patterns can be done

ABOVE: Contemporary designs like Lawana Poopoksakul's Hong Tao (Shophouse) collection help Mae Fah Luang's handwoven textiles blend into decor schemes around the world.

RIGHT: The late Princess Mother shared the King's devotion to sustainable alternative rural development. She launched the Doi Tung project in Chiang Rai at the age of 88, on the principle of "co-existence of man and forest". (Photos courtesy of Mae Fah Luang Foundation)

cover a large area, and establish best practices for use elsewhere in Thailand. Its aim was to help local communities address their own health, education and income needs while rehabilitating the environment. Tourism, handicrafts and new crops would be developed to raise income levels.

Crafts are a celebrated cultural asset of the local hill tribes, who over several centuries have migrated to Thailand from the Himalayas and other mountainous areas in southern China, Myanmar and Laos. Each tribe makes their own type of silver jewellery and colourful textiles for the women's regal daily garb. But the market for these handicrafts in their traditional form is small, not commensurate to the great skill, effort and time needed to make them. With this reality in mind, the Doi Tung project hired professional designers like Ploenchan Mook Vinyaratn in 1998 (page 134), and later Lawana Poopoksakul (page 138). They introduced patterns, colours and textures that would appeal to international tastes for fashion and interior fabrics.

The appeal has now been proven in design competitions and the marketplace. Mae Fah Luang's rugs, cushions, fashion fabrics and interior textiles fetch high prices. They also bolster the designs of local furniture makers like Yothaka and Planet, who use the fabric for upholstery. The foundation exports to markets like Italy, France and Japan. Its own boutiques in Thailand sell directly to retail customers. Every year, the brand commissions a different Thai women's wear designer to create a runway collection for Elle Bangkok Fashion Week, the nation's leading show.

Highland women still craft traditional designs for their own use as before, but weaving for Doi Tung enables them to make decent incomes. The hill tribes are also cashing in on new crops like macadamia nuts, flowers, cool climate produce and Chinese tea. They grow gourmet Arabica coffee for sale through supermarkets and Doi Tung's chain of cafés, which are bucking the global trend toward Starbucks.

People around Doi Tung have solved some of their chronic problems thanks partly to help from the project. Average per capita incomes in the area climbed from 3,800 baht per year in 1988 (then $147) to 30,700 baht in 2003 (then $775), or 123,000 baht per family. With 1,200 employees, the project's benefits spread to an estimated 11,000 people throughout the 150 sq kilometre district. The programme has helped quadruple the number of people there who have finished secondary school, while scholarships helped increase the number of college graduates from 18 to 183. Some 69 per cent of locals had obtained citizenship in 2003, up from 40 per cent in 1992. Infrastructure like telephones, electricity and fresh water supply have been installed. Forest cover has increased from 45 per cent to 80 per cent. Slash-and-burn farming and opium poppy cultivation have been eliminated. Mae Fah Luang has also established a Chiang Rai centre for studies of ethnic Tai culture covering the six countries where Tai peoples live. It opened the acclaimed Hall of Opium Museum to educate visitors on the social impact of world trade in illicit drugs.

Outcomes like these helped Doi Tung products earn certification from the United Nations Office on Drugs and Crime (UNODC). As the official label says, "The sale of this product contributes to the achievement of a drug free world. Through alternative sustainable development, villagers who once depended on opium production and use can now earn secure legitimate incomes by making these products."

The project's enlightened conception, professional management and good results prompted the United Nations to declare Doi Tung one of the world's most successful alternative development projects. MR Disnadda Diskul, the energetic man who heads the project, says Doi Tung succeeds because it focuses on sustainability, initiating activities that let local communities help themselves. The project will be wound down in 2017, when residents take over its operations completely.

Since 2002, Mae Fah Luang has gone international, working to benefit hill tribe communities in the Shan state of neighbouring Myanmar. It is also sharing information with groups in Afghanistan, today the world's largest source of illicit opium.

Years after the Princess Mother's death in 1995, she remains one of Thailand's most beloved public figures, as virtually ubiquitous display of her portrait in homes and businesses attests. In 2000, the United Nations Education, Science and Cultural Organization (UNESCO) named her a "great personality in public service".

Water Hyacinth
Crafting a Thai Solution to Colonial Weeds

Historians are apt to note Thailand's legacy of resisting conquest. The nation was the only one in South-east Asia that eluded Western colonisation, thanks in part to deft diplomacy. Yet Thailand did suffer one foreign invasion that continues to this day. Starting from a toehold in the 19th century, the interloper gained a chokehold on the lifeblood of Siamese agriculture, transport and commerce—the kingdom's myriad inland waterways. *Eichhornia crassipes*, the floating plant known as water hyacinth, still menaces canals, rivers and lakes.

Metre by metre, though, Thais are winning back lost territory by weaving the plants into furniture for export. It is a success story that started with an accident. Water hyacinth is native to the Amazon River basin in South America, where its lavender flowers and glistening leaves made it a favourite in the water gardens of European horticulturists. They took it to Asia in the 19th century, to the Dutch colony in Java. Among its admirers there were visiting Thais in the consort of King Rama V, or perhaps the King himself, who brought it back to decorate gardens in Siam, where the plant became known as *pak tob Java*, or Java grass.

It is beautiful in a garden pool or pot, but after escaping into the wild, the Amazonian's charms were unmasked. A botanist has called it "one of the world's worst weeds". A single water hyacinth plant generates enough seeds and sprouts to produce 3,000 offspring in 50 days. One hectare of water hyacinth can, in just eight days, become two hectares of water hyacinth. Over time, it forms a mat of floating foliage dense enough for a person to walk across. It blocks boats and snarls fishing nets. It steals sunlight and oxygen, menacing fish and native aquatic plants.

In the Amazon, the weed poses no problem—certain vegetarian fish and annual floods keep it under control. But in more than 50 countries elsewhere, the invading plant has no natural predators. Humans struggle to thwart it themselves. After the weed covered waterways in the southern United States, officials built mechanical crushers the size of houses. Fire was tried there, with little success. Explosives were worse. Bombing the plants simply blew them up into little green bits that sprouted afresh, producing explosive growth. Then there was an American scheme involving poison—spraying them with saltpeter—but cattle along the waterways liked the taste of it, with

A non-native species, floating *Eichhornia crassipes* brought Thailand little but clogged waterways until a 1980s research project innovated methods for turning the weed into furniture. (Drawing courtesy of the Center for Aquatic and Invasive Plants, University of Florida)

fatal consequences. Further south, Mexicans brandished bulldozers against it, ravaging the environment.

The Thais, however, fought back with creativity. First they tried turning the weed into pig feed. But for a pest that can double its population in a week, even pigs eat too little to help. So villagers crafted another solution: drying the stems to weave into baskets, hats, slippers and other small items.

In 1985, a group called the Association of Thai Women in Banking decided to initiate a rural development project to find ways to turn these humble crafts into something more. They hoped especially to make furniture, which would use enough weeds to help clear waterways and give rural women a needed source of income. Tapping a grant from the Canadian International Development Agency, the bankers funded a scientific study of the plant at Bangkok's Kasetsart University. They asked ML Pawinee Santisiri, known for her work as an interior designer, to help on the stylistic side of the project.

The effort quickly bore fruit. Scientists identified the best way to dry and preserve the water hyacinth stems. The stalks, just 50 centimetres long, were too short to make anything bigger than

baskets, so ML Pawinee decided to braid them. This produced cord sturdy enough for furniture. The project next recruited hundreds of villagers, who they trained and paid to produce braid. When enough braid was accumulated, ML Pawinee created a collection of chairs and accessories for public exhibition. The results were so good she invited a friend overseas to fly back to Bangkok and have a look. The friend—fellow interior designer Suwan Kongkhunthian, then working in Singapore—found it worth the trip.

"The moment I saw this material, I thought it was interesting—it had an attractive texture and colour," Suwan says. "We designers are always looking for something different, something new. I knew we could not let this drop." Suwan decided to move back to Bangkok and join ML Pawinee in forming a company to make furniture. Their early efforts stumbled, but by 1997 their designs had caught on in France and other countries in Europe. Now their firm, Yothaka, has some 200 employees, commissioning another 1,000 villagers to harvest, dry and braid the plants (page 32). They set up a second firm, Ayodhya, to make ML Pawinee's designs for vases, mats and other woven accessories (page 84).

Their firms consume more than 8,000 kilometres of water hyacinth braid a year—enough to stretch from their workshop to Paris. Thousands more kilometres are used by another dozen smaller firms that have followed their lead. Good riddance to the weeds, which are actually becoming scarce in some areas. That makes water hyacinth crafts doubly green. They're infinitely renewable, and no harmful chemicals are used to process the plant—just a food preservative that prevents mould.

Water hyacinth has become popular thanks to its special qualities. Because the stems are thick, the braid is wide, with a more rustic, masculine look than other woven fibres. Unlike rattan, which is shiny and brittle, water hyacinth is soft and flexible, with a porous surface that absorbs light, giving it a gentle glow. "Rattan cracks after you use it a few years, but water hyacinth absorbs moisture and breathes. I've been using my furniture for ten years, and the colour and texture are still very nice," ML Pawinee says.

This material's appearance conveys the climate and culture of South-east Asia because it shows it's been sun-dried. In one of the world's most sun-drenched regions, villagers take full advantage of natural solar energy to preserve their perishables, laying chillies and fish and shrimp in broad woven trays that are put outside in the day's blinding heat.

You can see this handicraft at its grassroots in rural Pathumthani province just 60 kilometres west of Bangkok. The landscape is classic central Siam—canals and sun-blasted rice fields dotted with palms and jackfruit trees, graceful White Egrets and other birds, stilted wooden farmhouses in blue, green, yellow and pink. Until the late 1990s, most villages here could only be reached by boat. The roads there now do double duty—on both sides they are lined with rows of hundreds of thousands of green plant

stalks—freshly harvested water hyacinth. After a few days in the sun, the stalks turn golden brown like rice crackers, now ready for braiding.

The farm families who braid stems here can earn a better living right at home without resorting to jobs in the congested city, just as the bankers had hoped. Prapai Saelee, for example, earns 5,000 baht a month for her family ($130), an amount that easily covers daily expenses and a few special purchases like a television and refrigerator. Sitting on a cushion on the floor of her simple wooden house, she braids while watching television and keeping an eye on her children. Often she works together with friends, the women competing among themselves and against other villages to see who can work fastest. Prapai is the local champion, pumping out 300 metres a day—almost twice the typical rate.

"My husband saw me working hard, so he bought me a washing machine," Prapai laughs. Her mother helps by gathering the plants in the nearby canals. With just four years of schooling—typical among rural Thais—Prapai says she wouldn't know what to do without water hyacinth.

Weavers in furniture factories like Yothaka's also benefit. Most used to farm, but earn more in furniture after just three months of training. Some continue to grow crops on the side, getting days off at planting and harvest time. In Europe or the United States, factory workers stand, or sit in chairs like clerks. Thai artisans prefer to sit on floor cushions or on ankle-high stools, the better to wrap their limber bodies around the furniture, cradling it with arms, legs and bare feet as they work. The craftsmanship is precise—weaving that is tight and even, handmade frames that stack up as neatly as machine-made goods. Says Yothaka's Suwan, "Thais have a gift for handiwork—it's something they are born with."

Creating a Vanguard
Artists Blaze a Modern Trail

Bangkok design is intertwined with Thailand's unusually vital modern art scene, which has invigorated furnishings in at least two ways. First, the nation's art colleges and universities have helped foster the human resources supporting design. Second, local artists have set stylistic and conceptual precedents that have suggested paths for design to follow.

In the decades following World War II, Thai artists began to explore modernism with newfound relish. Typically educated at Bangkok's Silpakorn University, the fine arts school established by Florentine sculptor Corrado Feroci in 1943, these painters, sculptors and printmakers worked in imported styles like realism, impressionism, abstraction and surrealism. But most of this work did not yet show a distinctively local character. Then in the 1960s and 1970s, Thawan Duchanee (page 64), Pratuang Emjaroen and a few dozen other artists began to develop modern styles that were truly Thai. Influenced by Buddhist iconography and ideas, they successfully adapted 19th-century mural painting and other local art precedents for use in contemporary expression. This neo-traditional approach was so successful, in fact, that it has become Thailand's official modern art style, decorating tycoons' mansions, bank lobbies and public spaces like Suvarnabhumi Airport.

Increasingly experimental work has prevailed since the mid-1990s, mostly in non-traditional formats like video, performance and gallery installations. While less obviously Thai in appearance, it often addresses matters of local importance like the cultural impact of globalisation. Overt Buddhist iconography is less common in this work, but much of it reflects thinking enriched by Eastern philosophy.

A pivotal figure in Thai art since 1990 is the late Montien Boonma, whose work abstracts the iconography of stupas, temple pavilions and sacred vessels. He created gallery installations that explore meditation, healing and the wish to transcend death—a response to his wife's demise from cancer in 1994 and the malignancy that would take Montien's own life in 2000. He draped a gallery in strands of aromatic Thai medicinal herbs, for example, expressing his yearning for wellness.

Others have carried on where Montien left off. Pinaree Sanpitak explores imagery of breasts and the female body as universal metaphors for human relationships and psychology. Montri Toemsombat does performances and installations that focus on meditation, rural culture and the implications of consumerism (page 150). Sutee Kunavichayanont's installations take sweetly

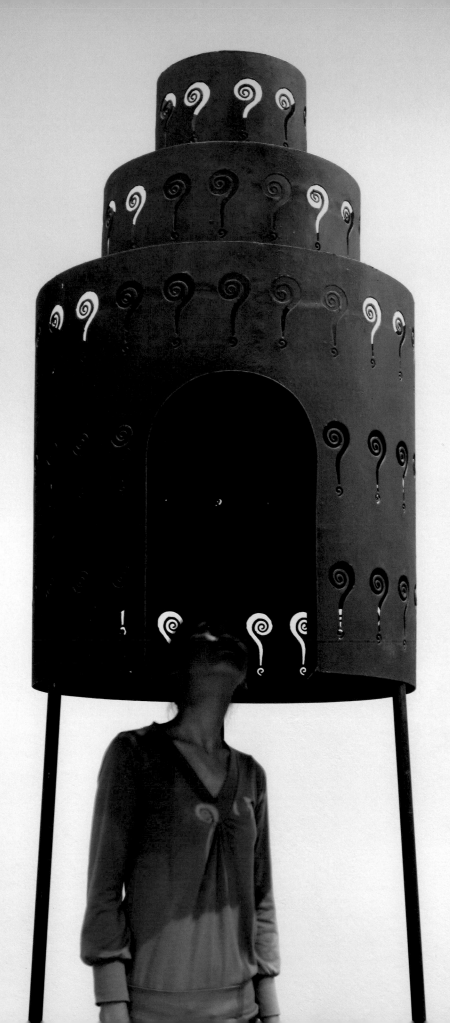

LEFT: **SALA OF THE MIND, 1995, BY MONTIEN BOONMA.** *Metal, sound.* In the wake of his wife's death from cancer, Montien envisioned gallery installations as sanctuaries for meditation and spiritual questioning. (Collection of Estate of Montien Boonma; photo courtesy of Office of Contemporary Art and Culture)

ABOVE: **HOUSE OF HOPE, 1996-1997, BY MONTIEN BOONMA.** *Steel grill, herbs, herbal medicine, mixed media.* The artist created a temple-like space of strands of thousands of prayer beads made of aromatic medicinal herbs, inviting audiences to transcend suffering through meditation. (Collection of Estate of Montien Boonma; photo courtesy of Office of Contemporary Art and Culture)

ironic looks at dilemmas of Thai identity. Trenchant political and social critiques feature in work by painter Vasant Sitthiket and conceptual photographer Manit Srivanichpoom.

Much of today's most acclaimed Thai art exists not as objects but as ideas and events. Rirkrit Tiravanija, Navin Rawanchaikul and Surasri Kusolwong have become known around the world for art projects that encourage participation and social interaction while blurring the lines between everyday life and a gallery show. Navin, for example, created a series of taxi-related work, about the universal urban institution of the car-for-hire. He installed a gallery of his work in an actual cab put in service in Bangkok from 1995 to 2000. Rirkrit, who has had shows at dozens of the world's leading museums and art expos since 1990, cooked up *pad thai* noodles in an influential series of gallery events.

Thai practitioners of abstract painting include Somyot Hananuntasuk, Somboon Hormtientong, Gumsak Atipiboonsin and Nim Kruasaeng (see endpapers, front and back).

A new generation of artists born in the 1970s show work that is charged by the energy of pop culture. Thaweesak Srithongdee, for example, offers accessible canvases bursting with Bangkok zeitgeist.

The vitality of Thailand's art scene—arguably the strongest in South-east Asia since the mid-1990s—owes a lot to the strength of fine arts education here. So does furnishings design. Local designers have more often studied decorative arts than industrial design, typically at Silpakorn. Among these talents are ML Pawinee Santisiri, Teera Morawong and many others. Suwan Kongkhunthian prefers to tap fellow graduates of arts faculties when he commissions or hires designers for his firm Yothaka. "They are more sensitive to aesthetics than ones who study industrial design," he says.

Local art schools graduate far more students of painting, sculpture and printmaking than local patronage can support as full-time artists. Among the alternative careers that graduates turn to is textile and furnishings design. And meanwhile established Thai artists themselves embrace design with a readiness unlike their counterparts in Europe and the United States. Western artists typically resist doing work that might be labelled 'decorative' or 'craft' because these are seen as lesser genres there. In contrast, Thais like Thawan and Thaiwijit have relished the creation of furnishings. Silpakorn painting graduate Udom Udomsrianan worked as an artist before becoming one of the strongest designers of furniture (page 42). Crossovers go both ways: Jakkai Siributr studied commercial textile design but abandoned it to focus on creating textile-based fine art (page 130). The hotel Reflections Rooms (page 158) celebrates the blurring of lines between art and design. Saiyart Semagnern (page 76) creates sculpture as well as art furniture, as did his sometime collaborator, architect Nithi Sthapitanonda (page 18).

If Thai art has helped inspire designers, it is fitting that design is now supporting art. The James HW Thompson Foundation, created after the American silk entrepreneur's disappearance, has become perhaps the largest non-government underwriter of Bangkok's art scene, hosting events and exhibitions at a new gallery built in 2004 at the Jim Thompson House Museum. Lighting designer Angus Hutcheson has commissioned local artists to decorate the Ango showrooms, and his brand features a line of furnishings by artist Thaiwijit. These precedents suggest that as other Thai design brands become established, they too will boost local art.

FURNITURE

Nithi Sthapitanonda (b 1948)
Architects 49 (www.a49.com)
Nithi studied architecture at Chulalongkorn University (BFA, 1971) and the University of Illinois, Urbana-Champaign (MFA, 1973). He joined Metcalf and Associates in Washington, DC in 1973, then Bangkok's Design 103 the following year. In 1983 he founded Architects 49, which has since become Thailand's largest architectural practice. A former president of the Association of Siamese Architects, Nithi was named a National Artist in 2003. He is co-author of *Architecture of Thailand: A Guide to Traditional and Contemporary Forms* (2006).

Ou Baholyodhin (b 1966)
Ou Baholyodhin Studio, London (www.ou-b.com).
Ou studied architecture at the Barlett School, University College London, furniture and product design at Kingston University (MFA), political science at London School of Economics, cookery in Florence and industrial design in Paris. At the London-based consultancy he founded in 1997, Ou Baholyodhin Studio, he designs products as well as residential and commercial interiors. Creative director of Jim Thompson since 2000, Ou has published two books, *Living With Zen* (2000) and *Being With Flowers* (2001).

Eggarat Wongcharit (b 1959)
Crafactor (www.crafactor.com)
Eggarat studied communications design at Silpakorn University (BFA, 1980) and New York's Pratt Institute (MFA, 1983) and industrial design at Milan's Domus Academy (MID, 1987). In Milan he worked for architect/designer Paolo Nava for two years before becoming an Italy-based freelance designer of furniture. From 1992–1999, Eggarat led the undergraduate industrial design programme at Bangkok's Rangsit University, where he launched and led an MFA programme from 2000–2006. He wrote a paper for the Gwangju Design Biennale 2005 exhibition book. He founded Crafactor in Bangkok in 2002.

Suwan Kongkhunthian (b 1949)
Yothaka International (www.yothaka.com)
Suwan grew up in Chiang Mai and studied interior design at Silpakorn University (BFA, 1976). After graduating, he briefly worked as a product designer for a Bangkok furniture manufacturer. He was an interior designer in Singapore from 1980 to 1989, before returning to Bangkok in 1989 to found Yothaka. He won the Best European Furniture Award at the Cologne Fair (1980), Japan's G-Mark (2003, 2004) and Hong Kong Design Centre's Design for Asia Award (2004) as well as many local honours.

Teera Morawong (b 1964)
Allure International (www.allureinter.com)
Teera studied interior design at Silpakorn University (BFA,1987) and the California College of Arts and Crafts (1989–91). He studied business at National University in San Diego (MBA, 1994), founding Allure in 2001.

Udom Udomsrianan (b 1956)
Planet 2001 (www.planet2001design.com)
Udom studied painting at Silpakorn University (BFA, 1985) and worked many years as a graphic designer and interior designer. He founded Planet in 1999 to produce his furniture designs. He won second prize for furniture in the *Elle Decoration* International Design Award competition (2003) and Japan's G-Mark Award (2003), as well as awards from *Elle Decoration* (Thailand) (2003) and Silpakorn University (2004).

Pisit Kunanantakul (b 1974)
Isolar Co. Ltd (www.isolar.co.th)
Pisit studied industrial design at Academy of Art College in San Francisco (BFA) and business management at London International College. He founded Isolar in 2001, and also runs GEM Car Asia, an importer and distributor of electric vehicles.

Apirom Kongkanan (b 1973)
Isolar Co. Ltd. (apiromkong@yahoo.com)
Apirom studied industrial design at San Francisco's Academy of Art College (MFA, 1999). She was awarded a scholarship from the Italian government to study at Academy De Belle Arti Di Brera in Milan in 2000. Twice a recipient of Honorable Mention Awards from the LG Electronics International Design Competition in Seoul (1997, 1999), her works were published in Germany's Vitra Design Museum summer workshop publication, 2004 and Brazil's *Casa e Jardin* magazine, 2004. In 2005, she began studies in Sweden.

Caryl Olivieri (1958-2004)
Artitude (www.artitude.co.th)
Born in Corsica, Caryl studied design in his native France, worked as a model and wrote travel guidebooks in Brazil, China and Taiwan. He came to Thailand in the mid-1990s as a jewellery designer for the Elle brand, and soon started designing gardens, landscapes, interiors and accessories. In 1998, he began making furniture for his own firm, Atmosfer and for the rattan specialist Artitude. He died from a fall in 2004 while tending the balcony garden in his high-rise apartment.

Swai Silpavithayadilok (b 1957)
Hygge (www.hygge.com)
A consultant to the maker of Hygge furniture, Swai is a reclusive figure who studied at Bangkok's Assumption College (BFA, 1976) and at Silpakorn University (MFA, 1980). He has worked as a graphic designer for Santoza Studio since 1989, and published a book of illustrations called *Somnambulist's Gallery* (2001).

Jitrin Jintaprecha (b 1976)
Consultant to Stone & Steel and other companies
Jitrin studied industrial design at King Mongkut's Institute of Technology, Ladkrabang (BFA, 2001). He has won several local prizes as well as Japan's G-Mark awards for four of his chairs (2005). A consultant designer, Jitrin has done collections for Stone & Steel (www.estonesteel.com), Corner 43 (www.corner43.com) and Hygge (www.hygge.com)

Thawan Duchanee (b 1939)
A native of Thailand's northernmost province of Chiang Rai, Thawan studied at Bangkok's Poh Chang art college (1955–57), at Silpakorn University (BFA, 1962) and for five years at Amsterdam's Royal Academy of Fine Arts (1964–1968). Thawan is best known for his paintings and drawings collected around the world, but is also accomplished as a sculptor and architect. He was named a National Artist in 2001 and won the Fukuoka Asian Cultural Prize the same year.

Chulaphun Chulanond (b 1963)
Existenze (xistnz@hotmail.com)
Chulaphun studied painting at Silpakorn University (BFA, 1984) and worked as an art director in magazine publishing and advertising before founding Existenze in 2000. His La Vie screen won Japan's G-mark award (2004) and a best of show award at the Birmingham Furniture Fair (2004).

Preeda Siripornsub (b 1972)
Innia Co. (www.inniadecor.com), Mobilia Flexy Living (www.mobiliaflexyliving.com)
Preeda studied interior design at Silpakorn University (BFA, 1997) and worked at P49 Design Co. for three years before creating Mobilia Flexy Living's first collection in 2002. He co-founded the Innia Co. furnishings firm in 2005.

Saiyart Semangern (b 1945)
Saiyart's Collection (www.saiyart.com)
Born in Siam's ancient capital of Ayutthaya, Saiyart graduated from Uthenthawai Building & Construction College in 1963. He began to exhibit his sculpture and furniture in 1989, and has had overseas shows in Amsterdam (2003) and Abu Dhabi, United Arab Emirates (2004).

ACCESSORIES

ML Pawinee Santisiri (Sukhasvasti) (b 1953)
Ayodhya (www.ayodhyatrade.com)
ML Pawinee studied interior design at Silpakorn University (BFA, 1976), and has been a practitioner since that time. Credited with helping pioneer the use of water hyacinth in furniture and other crafts, she co-founded Yothaka International in 1989 and Ayodhya Ltd. in 1995. She has twice won Japan's G-Mark Award (2003, 2004), a Grand Prize in Silpakorn University's Designer of the Year contest (2004) as well as the Overseas Award of the Tokyo Fashion Association (2004). In 2004, she organised a major exhibition and charity auction of royal handicrafts honouring HM Queen Sirikit's 72nd birthday and chaired the steering committee of the Thailand Creative and Design Center.

Sakul Intakul (b 1965)
Sakul Flowers (www.sakulflowers.com)
Sakul studied electronics engineering at King Mongkut Institute of Technology (BS, 1988) and flower arrangement at Manako Flower Academy. Among his awards are UNESCO's Seal of Excellence Award

(2003, 2004, 2005) and Japan's G-Mark (2005). He is co-author of *Tropical Colours: The Art of Living With Tropical Flowers* (2002) and *Modern Asian Living* (2005).

Gilles Caffier (b 1963)
(www.gillescaffier.com)
Frenchman Caffier studied applied art, textile design and fashion. He moved to Tokyo in 1984, where he taught fashion design and worked as a designer of fashions, interiors and textiles. In 1993, he relocated to Bangkok and opened a boutique to sell his own fashion and home decoration designs.

Angus Hutcheson (b 1955)
Ango (www.angoworld.com)
A native of Buckinghamshire, England, Hutcheson studied at London's Architectural Association (AA, 1981). He ran his own firm, Angus Hutcheson Architects, from 1984 to 2001 before co-founding Ango in Bangkok in 2002. His work has been exhibited at the Hara Museum, Tokyo and won two first prizes from *Elle Decoration* (Thailand) in 2003.

Thaiwijit Poengkasemsomboon (b 1959)
(thaiwijit@yahoo.com)
Born in Pattani province, Thaiwijit studied printmaking at Silpakorn University (BFA, 1984) and graphics at Akademia Sztuk Pieknych in Krakow, Poland (1985–1986). He has exhibited his paintings and prints in Asia, America, Europe and Australia. He was artist-in-residence at the University of British Columbia in 1990 and at the Thai Art Council in Los Angeles in 1991. He creates furnishings for his own studio and for Ango (www.angoworld.com)

POP & KITSCH ACCESSORIES
Vipoo Srivilasa (b 1969)
(www.vipoo.com)
Vipoo studied ceramics at Bangkok's Rangsit University (BFA, 1994), Melbourne's Monash University (1997) and University of Tasmania (MFA, 1998). His work is part of many public collections in Australia, and he has held nine solo exhibitions there and in Thailand. His work has won numerous awards in Australia, where he has lived since 1997.

Anusorn Ngernyuang (b 1962)
Reflections Thai and Reflections Rooms (www.reflections-thai.com)
Anusorn studied hotel management in Hamburg, where he worked for seven years before moving to Holland. During his eight years in Amsterdam, he ran three of his own Thai restaurants. He returned to Bangkok in the late 1990s to handle production for Czech designer Constantin Grcic before founding Reflections Thai. He launched Reflections Rooms in 2004.

Anurak Suchat (b 1972)
Aesthetic Studio (www.aesthetic-studio.com)
Chiang Mai native Anurak studied landscape architecture at Chulalongkorn University (BFA, 1994) and practised for several years before setting up his product design firm in 2000. He has won five local design awards, including a Grand Prize from Silpakorn University (2004) as well as prizes in Osaka's 'Rethink Consumption' International Design Competition (2003) and the National Lighting Fixture Design contest in the United States (2003).

Chaiyut Plypetch (b 1964)
Propaganda (www.propagandaonline.com)
Chaiyut studied visual communication design at Silpakorn University (BFA, 1987) and worked in advertising before becoming a product designer for Propaganda in 1995. He has won more international product design competitions than any other Thai designer, including awards from the Chicago Athenaeum Museum of Architecture and Design (2000, 2001, 2002) and Frankfurt's Tendence exhibition (2000, 2001) as well as a Red Dot Award (2002) and G-Mark Award (2002).

Satit Kalawantavanich (b 1959)
Propaganda (www.propagandaonline.com)
Creative director Satit co-founded Propaganda in 1994. He has had a busy career in advertising as well as product design. In 1988, he founded the Sam Noh Co graphic design agency and in 1991 launched the Phenomena TV commercial studio, which was ranked the world's most awarded firm in the industry in 2005 by the GUNN Report. He is a frequent speaker and judge at product design events. He has a BA in decorative arts from Silpakorn University.

TEXTILES
Tinnart Nisalak (b 1954)
Jim Thompson: The Thai Silk Co. (www.jimthompson.com)
Tinnart studied architecture at Chulalongkorn University (BA, 1975) and textile design at New York's Syracuse University (MFA, 1980). He worked for Jack Lenor Larsen Inc. in New York for two years before returning to Bangkok to join Jim Thompson in 1982.

Jakkai Siributr (b 1969)
(jakkaisiributr@yahoo.com, www.hgallerybkk.com)
Jakkai studied textiles at Indiana University (BFA, 1992) and Philadelphia University (MS, 1996). He has worked as an illustrator and columnist at several Bangkok magazines, including *House Beautiful*, where he was editor-at-large in 2004 and 2005. He has held several solo exhibitions in Bangkok and New York and was recipient of the Rockefeller Foundation's Bellagio Grant in 2001.

Ploenchan Mook Vinyaratn (b 1972)
Beyond Living (www.beyond-living.com)
Mook studied woven textiles at Central St. Martin's College of Art and Design (BA, 1995). She was senior designer for Mae Fah Luang (1998–2003) before founding Beyond Living Co. in 2003. She won a fabric design award from *Elle Decoration* (Thailand) (2004–2005) and a silver award in Silpakorn University's Designer of the Year competition in 2004.

Lawana Poopoksakul (b 1977)
Lawana Resort (www.lawanaresort.com)
Mae Fah Luang Foundation (www.doitung.org)
Lawana attended high school in the United States and studied textile design at Rhode Island School of Design (BFA, 2001). She joined Mae Fah Luang in 2001 and became chief textile designer before leaving in 2005 to work as a freelancer. She designed textiles and interiors for Koh Samui's Lawana Resort as well as the Villa Lawana, opening in 2008.

Sasiwan Dumrongsiri (b 1966)
Chabatik (www.chabatik.com)
Sasiwan studied decorative arts at Silpakorn University (BFA, 1988) and has been design director of her firm Chabatik since 1990. Among her awards are a first prize from the Ministry of Industry's Thai Silk Committee (1992), a scholarship from the Foundation of Asian Management in Japan, and a Grand Prize from Silpakorn University's Designer of the Year Awards (2004).

Jrumchai Singalavanij (b 1973)
Pasaya (www.pasaya.com)
Jrumchai studied industrial design at Chulalongkorn University (BID, 1996) and after graduation joined Pasaya's parent, Satin Textiles Co. He won the Trend Award at Belgium's Decosit Fair in both 2001 and 2002 and ranked among the first nominees in 2003 and 2004. He won a grand prize in Silpakorn University's Designer of the Year competition in 2004.

Worrachai Siriwipanan (b. 1975)
Pasaya (www.pasaya.com)
Worrachai studied industrial design at Chulalongkorn University (BID, 1998) and textiles design at Birmingham Institute of Art and Design in England (MA, 2001). From 2001 to 2003, he taught textiles design at Rajabhat Institute in Chiang Mai, joining Pasaya's parent, Satin Textiles Co. in 2004.

Montri Toemsombat (b 1975)
(montritsb@yahoo.com)
Born in Chaiyaphum province, Montri studied visual art at Chulalongkorn University (BFA, 1997). He has exhibited his work and performed in Thailand, France, Hong Kong, Japan, Australia, Singapore and Germany. He won the Young Designer Award at the Bangkok International Fashion Fair in 1999 and a Japan Foundation Fellowship in 2000.

CUSTOM DESIGN
Anusorn Ngernyuang
Reflections Rooms (www.reflections-thai.com)
See Pop & Kitsch entry.

Prima Chakrabandhu na Ayudhya (b 1980)
IceDEA (tib_prim@yahoo.com, wwww.icedea.net)
Prima studied industrial design at Chulalongkorn University (BFA, 2003) and Creamery Science at Kasetsart University. She worked as a product designer for Benchmark Studio and designed stationary for Bangkok's Mola brand (www.mola.co.th). In 2004, she established her ice cream consultancy IcedDEA before joining Benetton's design think tank Fabrica in Treviso, Italy in 2005.

OTHER FEATURED DESIGNS
Gumption Design Co. (page 184)
www.gumptionstyle.net

L Living (page 180)
www.l-living.com

Osisu (page 193)
osisudesign@gmail.com

So Fine (page 185)
www.sofine.co.th

GOVERNMENT & NON-PROFIT ORGANISATIONS
Chanapatana International Design Institute
www.chanapatana.com

Doi Tung Development Project (of Mae Fah Luang Foundation)
www.doitung.org

Department of Export Promotion and Product Development Center
www.depthai.go.th, www.thaitrade.com

Mae Fah Luang Foundation
www.maefahluang.org

Thailand Creative and Design Center
www.tcdc.or.th

TRADE SHOWS & ASSOCIATIONS
Bangkok International Gift and Housewares Exhibition (BIG) (bi-annually in April and Oct)
www.thaitradefair.com

Design and Objects Association
www.designandobjects.com

Furniture Industry Club (Federation of Thai Industries)
www.fti.or.th

Northern Handicrafts Manufacturers and Exporters Association (NOHMEX)
www.nohmex.com

OTOP—One Tambon One Product (Village crafts promotion)
www.thaitambon.com

Thai Furniture Industries Association
www.tfa.or.th

Thai Gifts, Premiums & Decorative Association
www.thaigifts.or.th

Thailand International Furniture Fair (TIFF) (annually in March)
www.thaitradefair.com

Thailand Textile Institute
www.thaitextile.or.th

ART GALLERIES
100 Tonson Gallery
www.100tonsongallery.com

Art Republic
www.artrepublic-bkk.com

H Gallery
www.hgallerybkk.com

Numthong Gallery
numthong_art_th@hotmail.com

Thavibu Gallery
www.thavibu.com

The Art Center at Jim Thompson House
www.jimthompsonhouse.com

The Queen's Gallery
www.queengallery.org

Surapon Gallery
sponglry@samart.co.th

MAGAZINES (Thai-language)
Art4D
www.art4d.com

Baan Lae Suan
www.baanlaesuan.com

Day Beds
www.daybedsmagazine.com

Elle Decoration Thailand
www.elledecor.co.th

Home & Decor
www.gmmultimedia.co.th

iDesign
www.isdesignmag.com

Room
www.roommag.com

Wallpaper* Thai Edition
www.wallpaperthailand.com

AUTHOR & PHOTOGRAPHER
Brian Mertens
www.brianmertens.net

Robert McLeod
www.robertmcleod.com

BIBLIOGRAPHY

Boym, Constantin, *Curious Boym*. Princeton Architectural Press, New York, 2002.

Cabra, Raul and Ngo, Dung, *Contemporary American Furniture*. Universe, New York, 2000.

Cornwel-Smith, Philip and Goss, John, *Very Thai: Everyday Popular Culture*. River Books, Bangkok, 2005.

Cranz, Galen, *The Chair: Rethinking Culture, Body, and Design*. WW Norton, New York, 1998.

Dormer, Peter, *Design Since 1945*. Thames & Hudson, London, 1993.

Fiell, Charlotte and Fiell, Peter, *Modern Furniture Classics: Postwar to Post-Modernism*. Thames & Hudson, London, 1991.

Greenberg, Cara, *Mid-Century Modern: Furniture of the 1950s*. Harmony Books, New York, 1984.

Hoskin, John, *Bangkok by Design: Architectural Diversity in the City of Angels*. Art Data, Bangkok, 1995.

Jumsai, Sumet, *Naga: Cultural Origins in Siam and the West Pacific*. Oxford University Press, Singapore, 1988.

Kunavichayanont, Luckana, *Thawan Duchanee: Trinity*, exhibition catalog. The Queen's Gallery, Bangkok, 2004.

Mertens, Brian and Sthapitanonda, Nithi, *Architecture of Thailand: A Guide to Traditional and Contemporary Forms*. Thames & Hudson, London, 2006.

Miller, R. Craig, *US Design 1975-2000*. Prestel Verlag, Munich, 2001.

Peleggi, Maurizio, *Lords of Things: The Fashioning of the Siamese Monarchy's Modern Image*. University of Hawaii Press, Honolulu, 2002.

Pettifor, Steven, *Flavours: Thai Contemporary Art*. Thavibu Gallery, Bangkok, 2003.

Poengkasemsomboon, Thaiwijit, *Rapture by Thaiwijit*, exhibition catalog. Vis-Art, Bangkok, 2001.

Poshyananda, Apinan *Modern Art in Thailand: Nineteenth and Twentieth Centuries*. Oxford University Press, New York, 1992.

Prasasvinitchai, Utong, *For Eyes That See: An Alternative Reading of Thai Mural Paintings*. Stock Exchange of Thailand, Bangkok, 2003.

Schoeser, Mary, *World Textiles*. Thames & Hudson, London, 2003.

Silpavithayadilk, Swai, *Somnambulist's Gallery*. Santoza Studio, Bangkok, 2001.

Warren, William, *Jim Thompson: The Legendary American of Thailand*. The Thai Silk Co, Bangkok, 1983

Warren, William, Beurdeley, Jean-Michel and Tettoni, Luca Invernizzi, *Jim Thompson: The House on the Klong*. Archipelago Press, Singapore, 1999.

Wongchirachai, Paravi, Phadungruangkij, Kowit and Yongvikul, Montinee, *Isan Retrospective: Deprivation, Creativity and Design*, exhibition catalog. Thailand Creative and Design Center, Bangkok, 2005.

SOURCES BY CHAPTER

Introduction, pages 10–15
Dr Aurapin Pantong, *A Study of Thai Characteristics as an Application for Jewelry Design*, Chulalongkorn University, Bangkok,1999.

Teera Morawong, pages 38–41
Greenberg, Cara, *Mid-Century Modern*

Swai Silpavithayadilok, pages 56–59
Miller, R. Craig, *US Design 1975-2000*
Swai Silpavithayadilok. *Somnambulist's Gallery*.

Thawan Duchanee, pages 64–67
Thawan is cited by:
Luckana Kunavichayanont in *Thawan Duchanee: Trinity* and Khetsirin Knithichan in *Mystique of the Master, The Nation*, October 17, 2004.

Flowing Lines, pages 172–173
Sumet Jumsai, *Naga*.

Colour, pages 174–175
Philip Cornwel-Smith and John Goss, *Very Thai*.

Sanook, pages 186–187
Pen-Ek cited by Aditya Assarat in *A Conversation with Pen-ek Ratanaruang, Director of Last Life in the Universe*. Asia-Europe Foundation website, http://sea-images.asef.org, 2003.

Readymades, pages 188–189
Constantin Boym, *Curious Boym*.
Paravi Wongchirachai, Kowit Phadungruangkij and Montinee Yongvikul, *Isan Retrospective*.

Animal Motifs, pages 192–193
ACNielsen research cited by Rob Walker in *Animal Pragmatism, New York Times*, April 23, 2006.

The Mosaic Method, pages 194–199
Eggarat Wongcharit, *The Hidden Treasures; Crossing over the borderline of local production*, paper published in exhibition book of Korea's Gwangju Design Biennale, 2005.

A Legend Grows, pages 202–205
William Warren, *Jim Thompson*.

Water Hyacinth, pages 210–213
Drawing and information on water hyacinth from Center for Aquatic and Invasive Plants, University of Florida, http://aquat1.ifas.ufl.edu

Creating a Vanguard, pages 214–217
Apinan Poshyananda, *Modern Art in Thailand*.
Steven Pettifor, *Flavours: Thai Contemporary Art*.

Bangkok designers certainly put their hearts into their work. Since the very beginning of this project, it was evident that they are doing it for love. Thanks to them, writing this book too became a labour of love. They and their colleagues helped in the labour, going beyond even the high level of patience and helpfulness that is customary in Thailand to assist with ideas, information and photography. Heartfelt thanks to all of these people.

Thanks are especially due to Suwan Kongkhunthian and ML Pawinee Santisiri, pioneers of water hyacinth design, who were always generous with their inspiration, advice and time. Many thanks too to Eggarat Wongcharit, the designer and former academic who has studied the Thai furnishings design scene more than probably any other individual.

Grateful thanks to photographer Robert McLeod who lavished attention to the shoots in a way that furnishings rarely if ever get. Few publishers give such sympathetic treatment to this field; many thanks to Marshall Cavendish's veteran design editor Melvin Neo and his graphic design colleague Lynn Chin whose ideas, discernment and dedication did so much to shape the book.

All of us who are either practising design in Bangkok or writing about it owe a debt to Dr Pansak Vinyaratn, who as chief advisor to the prime minister was the first such eminent government official to recognise Thailand's potential to excel in this field. Better, he did something about it by founding the Thailand Creative and Design Center. His ideas and comments helped inspire this book, as did those of his TCDC colleagues, especially Chaiyong Ratana-ung-goon and Paravi Wongchirachai. Three leading design professionals shared invaluable insights: interior designer and curator Chatvichai Promadhattavedi, architect Duangrit Bunnag and Greyhound fashion chief Bhanu Inkawat. Thanks too to furniture pioneer Prutipong Kijkanjanas of Stone & Steel, whose fine work is not included here simply because most of it preceded the current Bangkok design. I'm grateful as well for special help and insights from Angus Hutcheson, Tay Hiang Liang and Schle Woodthanan.

Special thanks to MR Disnadda Diskul, Khunying Puangroi Diskul na Ayudhya and their colleagues at Mae Fah Luang. At the Thai Silk Co., many thanks to Bill Booth, Surindr Supasavasdedhandu, Eric Bunnag Booth, Mai Vejjajiva, Chutima Pengsut and so many other helpful people. Thanks to ML Kathathong Thongyai and ML Paskorn Abhakorn and their colleagues at the Product Development Center, Department of Export Promotion.

Several curators and galleries helped with information, images and photoshoots. Many thanks to: The Queen's Gallery; Ek-Anong Phanachet of 100 Tonson Gallery; Gridthiya Gaweewong; Japan Foundation; Jorn Middleborg of Thavibu Gallery; H Ernest Lee of H Art Gallery; Claire Chatikavanij of Art Republic; Surapon Bunyapamai of Surapon Gallery; Chatiya Kate of Chulalongkorn University; and Dr Apinan Poshyananda and Alisa Bhoocha-oom of the Ministry of Culture. For allowing use of photos of their work, thanks to artists Chartchai Puipia, Manit Sriwanichpoom, Pinaree Sanpitak, Sutee Kunavichayanont, Thaweesak Srithongdee and Nim Kruasaeng.

Thanks to Twin Palms Resort; Robin Lourvanij of Kuppa Tea & Coffee Traders; Thammaroj Aksharanugraha of Jerlot Coffee Space; and Chawalit Suwathikul of TOA Paint, all for photo locations. Thanks as well to Peam Chongtaveetham and his parents Nui and Siem for a photo shoot at their home. Many thanks to two professors, Dr Utong Prasasvinitchai and Dr Aurapin Pantong. Thanks for interviews and other help to Art4D's Pratarn Teeratada; Kris Kiattisak and Jeremy Langford of Wallpaper*; and Gretchen Worth of BK Magazine. The magazines Baan Lae Suan, Day Beds and Elle Decoration (Thailand) were constant sources of inspiration and information, as were The Nation and Bangkok Post newspapers. Personal thanks to Mit Jai-in, Pakawee Wongsuwan, Angkrit Ajchariyasophon, Andrew Criswell, Dr Apichart Intravisit, Pongsai Kunarak, Chai Jeam-amornrat, Sareena Sernsukskol, Philip Cornwel-Smith, Poj Prommetta, Claudia Bieri, Carole Stevens and Elaine Ng. Deepest thanks to my parents.

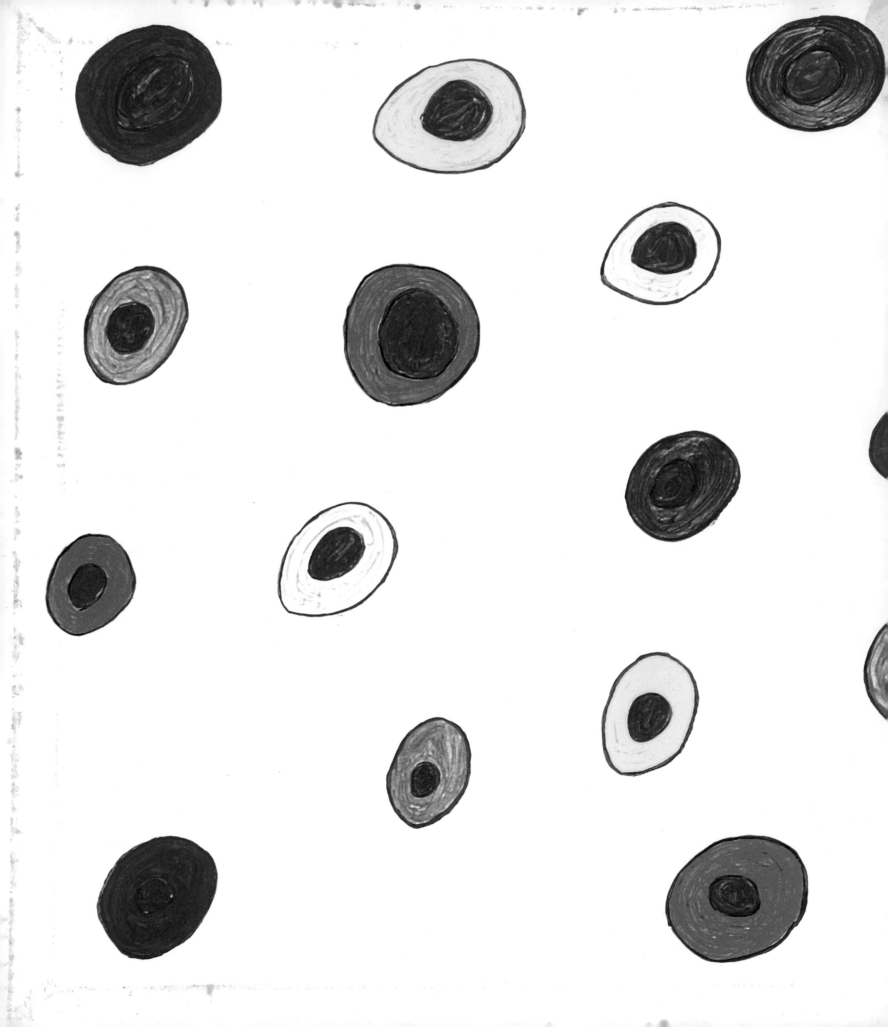